The creative and innovative power of a Genius

BY DR. SUNDAY ADELAJA

Sunday Adelaja

THE CREATIVE AND INNOVATIVE POWER OF A GENIUS

©2017 Sunday Adelaja

ISBN 978-1-908040-60-2

Copyright © Golden Pen Limited

Milton Keynes, United Kingdom. All rights reserved

WWW.GOLDENPENPUBLISHING.COM

This book or parts thereof may not be reproduced in any form, stored in a retrieval system, or transmitted in any form by any means — electronic, mechanical, photocopy, recording, or otherwise — without prior written permission of the author.

Cover design by Oleksander Bondaruk

Interior design by Oleksander Bondaruk

© Sunday Adelaja, 2017,
The creative and innovative power of a Genius — Milton Keynes, UK:
Golden Pen Limited, 2017

All rights reserved.

CONTENTS

PREFACE · 5

INTRODUCTION · 7

CHAPTER · GENIUSES ARE MADE NOT BORN 13
- A Look into the Lives of Few Geniuses 21
- Develop Your Genius Doing What You Love 27

CHAPTER 2 · GENIUS ABILITY WITHOUT WORK IS USELESS ... 33
- Academic Prowess is not Synonymous to Riches 38
- Discover the Great Treasure in You through Work 43
- No Rain When There is No Man to Work 45

CHAPTER 3 · DO NOT WASTE YOUR GENIUS;
               DEVELOP YOUR NATION 51
- Do Not Kill Your Great Potentials 53
- Wrong Orientation and Value System Undermines National Development . 59
- Hardship Should Awaken Your Genius; Not to Kill It 65

CHAPTER 4 · DO NOT ABUSE YOUR GENIUS; INVEST IT 73
- The Story of Segun, the Genius 75
- The Genius of Nigerian Scammers 77
- Two Genius Hackers 79
- The Genius Blogger 81
- The Boko Haram Genius 84
- Tedo, the Genius Womanizer 86

CHAPTER 5 · THE THINKING POWER OF A GENIUS 95
- Worrying Versus Thinking 99
- Are You a Lazy Thinker? 104
- If You Are Not Thinking, Then You Are Assuming 112

CHAPTER 6 · THE STUDYING HABIT OF A GENIUS 125
- Show Me a Great Genius Who Does Not Study 131
- Self-Education Leads to Amazing Discoveries 141

CHAPTER 7 · HOW I DISCOVERED MY OWN GENIUS 147
- My Greatest Discovery 149
- Developing Yourself Makes You Stand in the Shoes of Great Men 158

CHAPTER 8 · ARE YOU A CREATOR, INVENTOR OR AN INNOVATOR? 167
- The Difference between a Genius and an Inventor 175
- The World is Full of Potentials for Discoveries 183
- You can become Honourable 187

CHAPTER 9 · CREATE, INNOVATE AND INVENT YOUR WAY TO WEALTH 195
- Activating Your Creative Genius Ability for Financial Growth 205
- From Small Beginnings Come Great Things 212

CHAPTER 10 · INTELLECTUAL CURIOSITY OF AN INVENTOR/ INNOVATOR 221
- The Curiosity of Isaac Newton 228
- Curiosity Meets Needs and Solves Problems 229
- The Curiosity of Leonardo Da Vinci 234

CHAPTER 11 · THE SOLITUDE SECRET OF AN INVENTOR/ INNOVATOR 243
- The Importance of Tranquility to Creativity 251
- The Best Place to Work is in Solitude 257

CHAPTER 12 · THE FERVENT TENACITY OF AN INVENTOR/ INNOVATOR 265
- Tenacity of Henry Ford 266
- Failure is an Opportunity 270
- Tenacity to Overcome Failure 273

FINAL THOUGHTS · 283

REFERENCES · 285

PREFACE

It is my belief and hope that through this book, a whole generation of innovators would arise on the continent of Africa and beyond. I have attempted in this book lay down the principles of how every single individual could become a genius and a creative innovator.

I am certain that some of my readers will question this postulate, but I want to ask you not to be in a hurry to stone me. Please take your time and have the patience to read through the whole book as meticulously as possible.

I don't have any doubt in my mind that each and every one of us are equally gifted both to create, innovate and become a genius. I am already very excited for as many as are holding this book in their hand because it is your journey into a new quality of life. A life where everything becomes possible, realistic and easy to do. I and the whole world will be waiting for those products that you will come up with as a result of reading this book the creative and innovative power of a genius.

This book is just one of the 50 books I am releasing as my present to the world on the occasion of my 50th birthday anniversary which is taking place on May 28th 2017. Congratulations! Go for the best! Go for all God has for you!

For the Love of God, Church and Nation.
Dr. Sunday Adelaja

INTRODUCTION

It is indeed a tragedy to see people who are awesomely and wonderfully made but showcasing themselves as members of an intellectually disadvantaged race. Why is it that people who were born with marvelous brains have gladly embraced and accepted the falsehood of being born as a person of an average intellectual capacity? Ignorance of the great treasures that people have within them have made them think that the Creator is partial; they think that only a few people are created specially and that the vast majority of the world population are condemned to an average life with little or no mental exploits.

If you have heard the word "genius" used and you think it has nothing to do with you, please open the pages of this book and you will find out that you have been absolutely wrong all your life. You will find out that everyone was created equally by the impartial Creator; we all have equal access to the best of resources in this world; nobody has more than seven days in a week and 366 days in a year. The people who are acclaimed to be geniuses have only understood the true meaning of WORK and they have applied themselves to it to cause a manifestation of the precious abilities within them.

If you read and understand the truths shared in this book, you will stop viewing people that do highly exceptional things as if they dropped down from heaven and were not born like ordinary men. There is nobody on this earth that does not have the genius capability within. There is no one who was not born with creative, innovative and inventive potentials. It is only unfortunate that a lot of people have been blind to the seeds of greatness within them, and have accepted the lowly and despicable life of an inferior generation as a norm. All it takes to become enlisted among the best creators, innovators, and inventors of this world is on the inside of you; your chance of discovering and manifesting them is just at the mercy of your dedication to work.

How would you feel, if at the end of your days on earth you get to realize that you have so much potentials, abilities, and talents in you but you never knew about it? Going to the grave with all the treasures within you should be something you vehemently disallow from happening; your great destiny as a shining star on this earth is only at the mercy of discovering the exceptional and amazing capabilities on the inside of you. No matter how much you have been despised by people around you, commitment to work will make your genius obvious to everyone. Edison had to drop out of school because he had a learning difficulty; Einstein didn't talk until he was four and people around him had termed him an idiot. However, each of these men turned their fortunes around and used the same genius ability (that nobody thought was existing in them) to touch the world as some of the most impactful scientists and inventors that ever lived. How did they do it? They understood the thinking power of geniuses; they knew that worrying and assumptions are not the same as real productive thinking. Edison brought out

Introduction

the best in him because he always saw failure as a blessing, and he went on to achieve extra-ordinary feats with his life.

It is one thing to have discovered the amazing potentials within you; it is another thing to understand the importance of developing it through hard work. Dr. Ben Carson was already condemned to a life of mediocrity when everyone regarded him as a dullard. He had a rare privilege of discovering that there was a great potential within him irrespective of the molestation and ridicule he suffered from his mates. He decided to commit himself to the hard work of studying until he became one of the top neuro-surgeons in the world. The uncommon abilities and potentials within you are of little or no use even if you have discovered it but not making conscious attempts to develop it to a height of extra-ordinary significance.

The world today is filled with people with unique abilities who, rather than use it to make the world a better place, ignorantly use it to perpetrate evil. In the end, these people end up in prison, or worse dead, and their abilities are forever lost without any benefit to the world. Our country has one of the most-challenged economies in the world, yet, thousands of youths run financial scams, so complex that the most advanced securities in the world find it difficult to successfully curb them. What a waste of genius potential! These young men have abilities that could be used to improve our country's finances but choose to abuse it. They have not learnt to invest their genius capability rather than abusing it. Hence, they got themselves on a path to a disastrous life. In the pages of this book are secrets on how the discovery and the understanding of your genius ability will help you avoid wasting it.

Lacking the knowledge that no ability is meaningless, many people have wasted their talents out of ignorance. You may not have the talent to be a genius mathematician or a genius scientist, but that doesn't mean you're totally devoid of ability. Many have been misled to believe that the only geniuses are the ones that excel in the school classrooms, and as a result, a lot of people have wrongly despised their talent. Julius loved to cook and was very good at it, however, because he didn't do very well at school, he concluded that he didn't have any talent. Years later, he read the story of a chef that is highly respected in the world over; and there and then, he knew that could have been him. Julius could have been a world-famous chef but he didn't because he didn't apply work to his ability; he wrongly discarded his ability and as a result, he failed to maximize his genius potential. In the pages of this book, you will come to find how academic ingenuity is just one of many abilities one could be endowed with. You will also find how important diligence is to harnessing whatever genius potential you have, be it academic or otherwise.

You already have great and amazing ability in you; all you have to do is use work to convert potential to reality. Without work, you're no different from a man that sits on a gold mine but refuses to dig it up and refine it. In this book, you will find out what the "geniuses" do differently and how these things contribute greatly to them showcasing their abilities in an unusual manner. You will learn how to 'mine' the gold, which is your potential. You will realize that poverty can only reign in your life if you choose not to create wealth for yourself by discovering and developing your genius ability, in addition to using the great invention

Introduction

of "work" to add tremendous value to your generation by creating, innovating and inventing.

Some people discovered their own genus ability right from their early childhood years but they never used it to achieve any accomplishment of notable significance. A genius that doesn't use his ability to make an impact on his country or on the world is living a wasted life. A genius who is a genius for being sake is not much different from a dullard, who has not discovered himself. So, how can you take a step further from just knowing that you are a genius? How can you develop your genius ability till you become an innovator like George Washington Carver or an inventor like Thomas Edison? How can your genius ability make you great? Or wealthy? What habits do these creators have that makes them more successful than many others that regard themselves as geniuses but fail to use their ability for anything tangible? The answers to these questions and many more will be provided to you via this book.

By not developing your genius potential through intensive hard work, you are not only depriving yourself of the benefits that come with it, you're also depriving your nation of your exceptional capability. By abandoning your talents in pursuit of a 'well-paying' job and living for your salary, you're limiting yourself and mortgaging your wonderful destiny for peanuts. If you are just living to survive, you're denying your world the benefits of the latent extra-ordinary capabilities and potentials within you. The more people start coming to terms with their genius abilities, and the more people work hard to develop their discovered potentials, the more glorious the destiny of our nation becomes.

The Creative and Innovative Power of a Genius

I can tell you that reading this book simply means you are embarking on a journey of life transformation. The way you look at geniuses, your attitude to problems and challenges, your mentality, your studying and thinking habits — all these will transform beyond your imagination. You will come to discover the role that curiosity plays in inventiveness, you will find out how being alone can many times be a good thing — how to use the power of solitude to add value to yourself and to your world. It will become evident to you that tenacity — both mental and physical — is a non-negotiable requirement for innovation and invention.

It is my hope that the lessons you will learn in this book will not only go a long way in improving your life but also help advance the lives of as many people as possible around you. If all the readers of this book will understand and judiciously practice the principles exposed therein, then there will be an emergence of the smartest, most inventive, innovative, and creative men and women of all times; then, it will only be a matter of time before our beloved country takes its place at the top. I congratulate you because reading this book is about to make you an amazement to your world.

CHAPTER 1

GENIUSES ARE MADE NOT BORN

We have lived in a world that has made many individuals believe that some people were just born so special, and that they are created with supernormal and exceptional capabilities that separate them from everybody else. Sometimes, people tend to imagine while questioning themselves in doubt about the origin of so-called geniuses: *"Are we all truly from the same planet, or there is something just really different in the make-up of these people that distinguishes them from the rest of the world?"*

It is a widely accepted notion that one cannot force himself to be a genius. While this belief is very true, there is an addition they make to it that is a misjudgment — they say *"It's either you are born with a genius capability or you are not"* How wrong! One of the greatest fallacies that have caused most damage on this earth is to say that only some few people are born with genius capabilities. This is what majority of the world population believe in, and this has caused many people to be chronically limited in life. A lot of people never come to the actualization of their true potential till they die because of a pervasive ignorance of this truth. I know this may unwittingly shock you but until you really discover the truth, you will not be made free.

The Creative and Innovative Power of a Genius

The purpose of this book is to show you that all humans were born with amazingly awesome abilities. We all have great potentials in us, the kind that this world has never seen before. It is true that you cannot force yourself to be a genius, and the reason is because you were already created to be a genius, you are not just going to become one. The seed is already in you; the only work you will need to do is to discover that genius ability in you and develop it to maximize the reason why you were created with it. Your work is to develop your mental ability from just seeing one thing to a level you can see so many things, and then your world will refer to you as a genius.

> *Genius is the capacity to see ten things where the ordinary man sees one.*
> Ezra Pound

I like to tell you about Brian who made an important discovery many years ago when he couldn't wait to listen to his highly revered idol. Brian was an ardent admirer of the generally appraised intellectual prowess of Professor Carl White. He could not believe he was seated in the hall about to listen to one of the best in his field. The common phrase in people's mouth was *"that man is simply a genius!"* Professor White had a story which was one of a kind. He started his school life impressing everybody who taught him. His parents had not known the kind of child they gave birth to, but soon, they found out. The A's that trailed him in his subjects from elementary school to high school all the way to college were enough to make them know their child was not ordinary.

Brian adjusted his seat, getting ready to listen to his role model; he made sure he came early to the venue so he could have the best view of his hero. The chairman of the day came forward and announced the reason for their being there. Professor White was launching a new book and many people were of the opinion that it was an academic book but they were about to get the shock of their lives. Without further ado, Professor White was invited to the stage. Not only was he a genius but he had a tall muscular frame. His genius intelligence was not the only fascinating thing about him, his height was too. Brian held the edge of his seat as Professor White's baritone voiced vibrated in the hall. He knew this was one experience he would not forget in a hurry.

Professor White looked all around the room. He could not believe two thousand people had turned up for his book launch. Well, today might be about the book to them, but to him, it would be more than that. It would be about the people seated in the room and sharing with them, words that can change the course of their destiny. It would be about letting them know there is so much inside them they haven't tapped yet. Wiping his glasses and putting them on, he started:

"Today, about sixty percent of you are here looking at me as a mini god; thirty percent think I must have some weird black magic powers because of my achievements. Five percent of you probably dislike me but still want to know more and the other five percent want to know my secret. Well, there is something all of you will learn here today. Something profound and propelling that it will change your life forever if you fully grasp it."

The Creative and Innovative Power of a Genius

"You all think you know my story but you don't. Let me tell you a little about my life. Growing up, I had good grades in high school. As one of the best students in Mathematics, Physics, and Chemistry, I represented my school in many competitions. Sometimes, I did it alone. Other times, I competed with other people. I won many awards. On my dresser, I had ten trophies when I graduated from high school. I was well known."

"University days came and I excelled just as much. I won a scholarship to study at the University because I had straight A's from high school. I graduated with First Class Honors. I also bagged my Master's degree from the same University with distinction grades"

"I was at the stage of my life where I wondered what was next. I knew most people seeking a doctorate degree finish it within four years but I told my friends I would finish it within three years. I put my mind to it and achieved it. I was at the pinnacle of my career and offers were pouring in for me. I had offers to work in reputable companies, many high-ranking universities, and multi-national organizations. I picked up a job with one of the companies but after a while, I knew I needed a change so I went for a research study in the field of vibration. I was awarded the degree of Doctor of Science, DSc. I was so in love with mechanical engineering that I looked around me and thought: "what can I do differently?" An idea came to me and I developed it. I successfully converted my family car from a right-hand drive car to one that can be driven in both right-hand and left-hand drive modes"

"All my achievements are good enough reasons for me to be happy, but there is a lingering dis-satisfaction in my soul every day. I have always wondered why people think my brain is so special; I see everyone referring to me as a genius. But I am convinced within me that I am no different than they are; How I wish that they can see the real difference between us."

> *Talent hits a target no one else can hit.*
> *Genius hits a target no one else can see.*
> ARTHUR SCHOEPENHAUER

I am sure everyone who referred to Carl as a genius has some form of talent buried within them. But because they had not developed their exceptional capability, they were not seeing with the eyes of a genius. Carl white was hitting great targets because he could see a difference between ordinary people and exceptional people in terms of the way they think. He continued his speech by saying:

"The major difference is just in the way we think. When others think something is cumbersome, I think I can break it down into simpler and much tinier steps and solve each chunk or unit one at a time. When I do it this way, I know it may take me time but I will eventually somehow achieve my purpose with time. This is the same principle I apply to any kind of subject I want to study. Even when I want to solve a problem, I break it down into several simpler and less complex problems, then I solve a tiny bit at a time. After doing this and I achieve a result that seems to be great to people, they start saying "we know you are Genius". I cannot count how many times I feel like bursting out in emo-

THE CREATIVE AND INNOVATIVE POWER OF A GENIUS

tions that seem to be uncontrollable in order to tell them we are all the same; that our brain is made equally, we only use it differently and with different approaches and styles. Each time I try to explain to people, they find it difficult to understand. But I sincerely do wish that everyone sees that there is nothing special about me."

"If you can think just the way I think and act the way I do, you can achieve comparable results. Likewise, if you can use your brain better than I use mine, you will getter better results than I get. The brain we have is a tool; the difference between you and I is that we use it differently. Instead of praising me and thinking I am a special genius, why not be curious enough to discover how I use my own tool better than you use yours?"

Carl White's expository speech as just related to you is an amazing one that can change your life forever if you grasp the concept he was talking about. Truthfully speaking, there are no people with inferior abilities and aptitudes; we only have people who have not discovered the amazing potentials within them and develop it to a level that we all refer to as the genius level. There is nobody who is correctly referred to as a genius in this world today who is not a hard worker, who meticulously breaks down great tasks into smaller steps to attack each one at a time. Can you show me anyone who continually makes great discoveries without an addictive habit of research and studying? Can you show me any student who is always the best in his or her class but does not read? But the world has continued to live in so much delusion, thinking that people with genius abilities are created differently, instead of attributing their great feats to their intensive efforts and systemic way of doing things.

> *Intelligence recognizes what has happened.*
> *Genius recognizes what will happen.*
> JOHN CIARDI

We should never forget the law of sowing and reaping; it applies in every aspect of life. You cannot plant cassava, and be expecting to reap tomatoes. Anyone who sows focused and intense study and meditation surely reaps an unusual level of understanding. In the same vein, if you sow laziness, inaction, and distractions, you reap confusion and frustration. Be not deceived — what you put into life is what you get out of it. Everyone who is seen as a genius today was not born that way, they have consistently sown the right seeds of hard work to get to and operate at the level we see them function. Friend, nobody is better than you; if you can just figure out the way they think and act, and you begin to think and act in similar or better ways, you will begin to accomplish comparable or even better results. John Ciardi rightly said in the quote above, most people usually see what has happened (i.e they only acknowledge a genius capability after it has been developed) but real geniuses recognize what will happen if they put in the required work to achieve a feat; they know that their world will stand in ovation for them if they pay the required price of diligence.

According to Merriam Webster Dictionary, a genius is *"a very smart or talented person: a person who has a level of talent or intelligence that is very rare or remarkable."* A careful look at this definition alone will let you know that

The Creative and Innovative Power of a Genius

Geniuses are not born; they are made. I am sure you are wondering "how come?" Okay! Can you tell of anyone who is very smart or highly talented, whose level of smartness and intelligence has been the same since he was born? No! If we have the same level of intelligence or smartness that we had when we were born, we would be seen as retards. We all grow in the use of our talent, smartness or intelligence. And if not deliberately developed, it does not grow. It just happens that the people who have been referred to as geniuses are ones who have excelled in developing their own abilities.

No matter how smart a person is, someone has to teach him the alphabets before he could learn it. Most of the things you know today, you learned them through studying, observation, or being taught by someone else. Therefore, it is when you develop your talent or intelligence in any aspect of life to an extra-ordinary level that people refer to you as a genius.

Very many years ago, the few people who could drive a car were regarded as a genius or extra-ordinary people because not many people had learnt how to drive a car. There was a time in human history when only few people could read and write, and such people were regarded as super-normal until the concept of the alphabet was discovered to make the learning of reading and writing an easier task. Imagine if there were not programs to develop the reading and writing abilities of people; imagine that the concept of driving school was not developed, reading, writing, driving that have become a common practice today would have still been seen as an ability that people are born with, not ones that can be acquired and developed to an expert level.

In today's world, an average person can drive a car; an average person can read and write, at least, in our civilized societies. This means that your willingness and determination to put in the necessary WORK to operate at a level beyond what is common and ordinary is what makes you enlisted in the league of geniuses. Now, get me very clearly — not that you are not already a genius, but if you are not dedicated to doing the right kind of work that you will be learning about all through this book, your genius capability will not shine forth to your world.

Put simply, the way we know and recognize geniuses in our world today is through the display of amazing talents and abilities. But how would anyone be able to display the special ability within if it is not first discovered? If the exceptional potential within is discovered and not developed, how would it rise to a level that is above the ordinary and supersede the commonly obtainable? Until you realize that it is only through WORK that you will be able to mine from the precious gold deposits of genius capabilities that you were created with; until you come to the knowledge of the fact that it is only through WORK that you will refine the rusty look of the amazing golden potentials you were packaged with by the Creator, your genius potential will not manifest, shine and be a center of attraction to your world.

A LOOK INTO THE LIVES OF FEW GENIUSES

There are so many people seen as geniuses in our world today, yet they constitute a very small percentage of the entire world population. We will be looking at the lives of some of these great people all through this book. But in this chapter, I like to start with Ufot Ekong, who is the Nigerian genius who solved a thirty-year old equation as part of a project under a confidentiality agreement, which his entire research team is not at liberty to discuss. To think that no mathematical expert has been able to, and a mere student did is a great achievement. And the most amazing news is he did it at the tender age of twenty years! According to a report by CCTV Africa, he graduated in 2015 as the best overall student with the best grades from a Japanese university — Tokai University in Tokyo. And it was said that the school had not recorded such a feat since 1965. This Nigerian speaks English, French, Japanese and Yoruba, his country's native language, and paid his way through university by himself.

Now, it is possible to just look at all the achievements of Ufot from the surface, and not realize the diligence that was involved. How many people would want to direct their energy at a problem that has remained unsolved for about thirty years? It takes diligence to begin to think that you want to do what nobody has done before. It takes a heart that is ready for hard work to attempt to solve a problem whose history is loudly announcing how tough it may be.

According to HuffingtonPost.com, Ufot Ekong built a car with his classmates in his final year in school. He won a Japanese language award for foreigners, and currently, he has two patents for electronic cars to his name. He recently built a car that can go as fast as 128 kilometers per hour. His success did not happen overnight. He discovered his genius ability when he won a Japanese Speech Contest. He realized he could be more than what he was. He decided to log in extra studying time so he could achieve more and more with his time.

It is important to note that the discovery of your genius capability will start with a heart that is ready to work and achieve results. Anyone who wants to attempt great things will not allow the fear of failure hold him down. One of the principal ways to keep discovering your genius capabilities is to have a mindset that chooses to continually determine to do what no one around you has been able to do; developing a mindset that is not afraid of failure at attempting new and greater tasks will let you unleash the hidden potentials within you.

The next person I want to tell you about makes people open their eyes in amazement when they hear about her story. She is young Esther Okade whose mother discovered her genius ability at the age of three when she started school. It was discovered that she could solve supposedly difficult mathematical questions without batting an eye. Esther had been silently unleashing her love for math in quiet studies. Her parent decided to motivate her to grow her talent. And according to CNN (2015), the talented 10-year-old enrolled at the Open University, a UK-based distance learning college, and was already top of the class, having recently scored 100% in a recent exam.

Are you beginning to see clearer that it takes conscious efforts and attempts to grow one's ability after being discovered? If nothing is done with the abilities that the Creator gave us, nobody will ever get to know that we can do exceptional things. If Esther's ability had not been developed through motivation and encouragement, she would have ended up like many other kids at ten years old, who are still trying to learn how to do simple multiplication.

Now, I need to let you know that geniuses are not only those that gain admission to study at a young age or individuals that break academic records. Developed geniuses are people who are usually at the top in their fields or career regardless of whether they passed through the formal educational system or not. They rank far above others who are in the same calling or profession with them notwithstanding the amount of disabilities or disadvantages in their lives. Therefore your age should not be a deterrent factor; you should never think that you are too old to discover the super-normal ability within you. In the first place, what makes old people not very much useful in our world? It is simply disability and incapacitation. But many people have proven that genius ability can shine through the barriers and limitations of disability.

One of such people is Stephen Hawking who suffered many disadvantages that should have stopped him from putting in the work to develop his genius ability and instead render him useless. But he wisely allowed his incapacitation to spur him to develop the great treasure he had found in himself to a height that cannot be ignored by his world. He is an English theoretical physicist, cosmologist, author, and Director of Research at the Centre for Theoretical Cosmology in the University of Cambridge. His genius ability was discovered when he was in high school; He and his friends, with the help of their math's teacher, built a computer from clock parts, an old telephone switchboard, and other recycled components. Knowing he could do this helped Stephen develop a sense of self-worth. He knew that if he could build that, there was so much inside him he had not even tapped.

When Hawking was twenty-one years, he was diagnosed with a slow form of amyotrophic lateral sclerosis (ALS). His physical abilities deteriorated. He could not write anymore, let alone feed himself. He could not put coherent sentences together as well. He was more or else unable to do basic things human beings could do. However, this did not deter the development of his genius; instead, it fostered it. I honestly believe you do not have any excuse not to develop your genius potential to a point that the whole world will acknowledge it as a blessing.

Hawking, in his handicapped state, has been able to prove and disprove many scientific theories; he has written and co-written many books on physics. The number of awards he has won in his lifetime also goes to show he is at the top of his career. In 2015, he won the BBVA Foundation Frontiers of Knowledge Award. In 2012, he won the Fundamental Physical Prize. In 2009, he was the recipient of the Presidential Medal of Freedom. Therefore, permit me to say that it is not any kind of limitation that lets anyone remain a dullard or an average person; it is a personal choice to develop yourself that makes you be regarded by all as a genius.

Geniuses are seen to operate at a level that is beyond the ordinary; they show extra-ordinary abilities in their fields of endeavors. They might not make the news every day, but they are making waves in their fields. In recent times, the use of solar energy has slowly gained some popularity in Nigeria; We have none other than Professor Emeritus Alexander Animalu to thank for this. He won a scholarship to study in University and he graduated top of his class. One of the events that confirmed the discovery of his genius ability was when he won Faculty of Science Prize for the best performance for two consecutive years in University. He then went ahead to develop it by spending more time doing a lot of research. He had a dream to publish one of the best books that could be referred to in his field. He achieved this when he bagged his Ph.D. (Maths) in Theoretical Solid State Physics. People just look at Emeritus professors as if their own brains dropped from heaven. What most people fail to see is the love and dedication of these people to their work. If you are so committed and devoted to hard work, what else will you get apart from super-normal accomplishments? We were all given brains equally by the Creator; all that is left for us to do is to use it so profoundly to produce maximum results. You cannot expect someone who is busy playing in trivialities around and whiling away time to achieve comparable results to the achievement of someone who is as loyal to his calling/profession as he is devoted to hard work.

The quality of Animalu's thesis was so high that the main results were published in the Philosophical Magazine in 1965 and included in W.A. Harrison's book entitled "Pseudopotentials in the Theory of Metals". He could have only achieved this feat through no other means than diligence, dedication, and devotion. Later, he made a proposal to the Federal Government of Nigeria for the establishment of a Centre for Energy Research and Development at the University of Nigeria, Nnsuka (UNN) in 1980. His proposal was accepted. In 1990, he was given the title "Ahiajoku" lecturer which is the highest academic privilege given to

Igbo Scholars. Professor Animalu was able to prove beyond reasonable doubt that it is possible to exhibit extra-ordinary abilities in any field of one's endeavor. His results have shown that nobody was born as a professor; everyone works hard to become one. In the same vein, nobody is born as a genius, you work hard to develop your own ability so you can be recognized as one.

DEVELOP YOUR GENIUS DOING WHAT YOU LOVE

Reading about the lives of these geniuses, don't you think there is something inside you that can make you exceptional in life? Don't you think you have more to offer to the world than you are doing presently? The truth is everybody has talent; everybody has unique potentials. But are you ready to discover and develop yours? Think about this for a second: what will you be known for? What will be your genius ability everybody will refer to? Although, you are already a genius but the world will not just bestow the word "genius" on you. You have to work hard for it. You also can be seen as a genius if you do what you love and you work hard until you become extremely good at it.

Tara Fela-Durotoye is an example of someone who was just busy doing what she loved, and now, people call her a genius in the make-up and fashion industry. She did not start her life thinking about makeup. In fact, she studied Law as an undergraduate. She started out by interning at a make-up outfit while waiting to gain admission into the university. She saw that she was quite good with people's faces so she invested in the business. Her breakthrough came when she did a make-up for one of her friends that was a naval officer for her wedding. Many offers poured in for her afterwards. As of today, she has a make-up studio named "House of Tara" where she trains and mentors many young women to discover their hidden talents. A lot of people today enroll in her school because they want to become makeup geniuses as well. Do you know what makes Tara's story unique? She worked on the ability inside her to make herself exceptional. She didn't know making up people's faces would make her a beauty genius; she was just busy doing what she loved and what she had discovered she had a unique potential to do. She had no idea she was a genius or that people would call her a genius when she started but today, her hard work at developing her ability to become extra-ordinary has paid off.

Many more people are in the world today, doing what they love in their areas of interest and they are excelling at it. We will be delving into more of them throughout this book. Some of them may not have a heavy presence on the internet or have long epistles written about them but they are geniuses. It is high time you also discovered your genius potential that you have always carried inside of you; it does not have to start and end with academics. Most of the time, genius ability or potential is mostly related to what you love doing and things you are very passionate about. It is always easier to develop a gift you love using as a hobby or even in a venture that you don't care much about being compensated for it. Think deeply: What do you love doing? What makes your soul light up when you are doing it? Keep in mind that it's not all about your IQ. Being a genius is a combination of hard work, IQ, talent, skill, determination, and patience. If you have a combination of these, you are well on your way to shinning as a star genius to your world!

I have made an attempt in this chapter to lay a good foundation that shows you that nobody was born as extra-ordinary; we were all born with genius potentials but until we discover such talent within us and develop it to a level that is beyond the common, the world will not start seeing and acknowledging us as geniuses. Now you know that it takes hard work for your genius ability to be able to shine forth. In the next chapter, I will be showing you that you need to push yourself beyond limits through diligence in order to discover and develop your genius potentials. Or else, it will remain useless.

GOLDEN NUGGETS
FROM CHAPTER 1

1. It is true that you cannot force yourself to be a genius, and the reason is because you were already created to be a genius, you are not just going to become one.

2. The major difference between ordinary people and geniuses is in the way they think. When others think something is cumbersome, a genius breaks it down into simpler and much tinier steps and solve each chunk or unit one at a time.

3. Instead of praising geniuses and thinking they are special, be curious enough to discover how they use their own tool (brain) better than you use yours.

4. Truthfully, there are no people with inferior abilities and aptitudes; we only have people who have not discovered the amazing potentials within them and develop it to a level that we all refer to as the genius level.

5. Anyone who sows focused and intense study and meditation surely reaps an unusual level of understanding. In the same vein, if you sow laziness, inaction, and distractions, you reap confusion and frustration.

6. We all grow in the use of our talent, smartness or intelligence. And if not deliberately developed, it does not grow. It just happens that the people who have been referred to as geniuses are ones who have excelled in developing their own abilities.

7. It is only through WORK that you will refine the rusty look of the amazing golden potentials you were packaged with by the Creator.

8. One of the principal ways to keep discovering your genius capabilities is to have a mindset that chooses to continually determine to do what no one around you has been able to do; developing a mindset that is not afraid of failure at attempting new and greater tasks will let you unleash the hidden potentials within you.

9. We were all given brains equally by the Creator; all that is left for us to do is to use it so profoundly to produce maximum results. You cannot expect someone who is busy playing in trivialities around and whiling away time to achieve comparable results to the achievement of someone who is as loyal to his calling/profession as he is devoted to hard work.

CHAPTER 2

GENIUS ABILITY WITHOUT WORK IS USELESS

Tayo Eket alighted from the commercial motorcycle in front of his father's house, and he sighed in exasperation. "What am I going to do with my life?" he wondered silently; Tayo was a twenty-two year old secondary school dropout. Right from time, he had never enjoyed going to school, but he went because he was expected to; where he grew up, children had to go to school, no exceptions. A dropout at 22, he was ashamed to walk around the neighborhood. Everywhere he looked, he found his former classmates; many of whom had already graduated, some even had jobs already. Even though they wouldn't out rightly mock him, their *"What are you doing now, Tayo,"* questions were enough to remind him of how bleak his future looked. He could see the mockery in their eyes as they asked the question; after all, they all called him "Tayo Olodo" meaning "Tayo the dullard" when they were in secondary school.

In front of his father's house, Tayo stood and shuddered at the shame and embarrassment he had faced over the years. He flashed back to his experience in primary four. He had failed again and had to repeat the class. His class teacher was astounded as to what went on in his mind; she had never seen any student as mentally backward as him before. She was curious as to his future plans; how did he plan to make it in life? What does he intend to become in life? She was stunned when Tayo 'the dullard' told her he aspired to be the most influential man in his community. She resisted the urge to laugh out loud, "funny kid!" she thought to herself as the other students around her laughed hysterically. This and many other episodes like it were scorched in Tayo's memory; people had always mocked him because of his supposed inferior intellect.

Tayo stood at the spot the motorcycle man dropped him off and stared blindly at his father's house, he didn't feel like going in. He had just checked his third UME (University Matriculation Examination) result, and unfortunately, it was worse than the previous two. His father had told him he would have to learn carpentry if he failed. Tayo thought to himself, "I cannot face my father like this." He turned from his house and decided to go to his uncle's; he knew his uncle would take him in without much judgement. As Tayo expected, his uncle was delighted to have him.

Days later, Tayo sat idly in his uncle's house and without paying mind to it, he got a pencil and a drawing book. He found himself drawing different types of upholstery and dining table sets, and he was surprised to realize that he had some creativity in putting together unique furniture. Definitely, his father must have also discovered he had some gift in carpentry work. Some days later, he took his designs to a carpentry workshop and told them to craft it out; they told him that they couldn't because they had never done anything of such before. Tayo went back home disappointed. On seeing his demeanor, his uncle asked him what was wrong, Tayo explained his predicament and showed him some of his drawings. His uncle was amazed and he could hardly believe that his nephew was so talented. "You have to learn carpentry," he said. "I don't want to be a carpenter," Tayo retorted, "in fact, that is the main bone of contention between me and my Dad." His uncle sat him down and made him understand the uniqueness of his designs; "Tayo," his uncle said, "You are the only person that can bring these designs to life but first, you must learn how to put the woods together. If you don't, you'll never find a carpenter that will do these drawings justice." After some persuasion, Tayo reluctantly agreed and that was the turning point in his life. He worked hard and all the hardship he faced while growing up made him even more determined to succeed. In less than a year, Tayo was able to construct some of the most beautiful types of furniture ever produced in the nation; that was the beginning of his success.

The most interesting part of the story is that — fifteen years later, Chief Tayo Eket was back in his home town. He smiled as he noticed it was the same spot the bike man dropped him off the day he left home for good. He noticed the people from his town waiting to receive him, even in front of his father's house. Tayo was now a big shot, he owned the biggest furniture house in the country and he was in town to officially launch his Aid and Scholarship program for the people in his hometown. Since he was doing so well, he wanted to give back by helping the less privileged. On his way to the venue, Tayo was shocked to see many of his classmates among the people who came to receive him, none of which anybody is hearing their names. He wasn't just richer than they were, he was also more influential and he had more impact on their community than they could ever hope to have. They were the geniuses then, but today, Tayo was the successful person; Tayo wondered as to why their lives turned out so, "they probably didn't put in the necessary work" he said to himself," they thought that having intellectual genius automatically translates to wealth" he mused with some pity.

Tayo made the greatest discovery of his life when all hopes of trying to excel in academics were lost. He had no other thing to work on but the despised furniture business. He decided to brace himself and put in everything necessary to make sure he could be as much of a success as he could possibly be. But in the process of putting in so much work into his vocation and business, he realized that there is nothing like an irrelevant or inferior ability. All kinds of abilities can be developed to the genius level; the only thing required is to put in the necessary diligence. Then, it became clearer to him that academic genius is just one of the many genius abilities people can possess. There are many other fields that may not be even taught in school but people can discover they have exceptional talents for creativity or discoveries in such areas. Through work, he developed a new philosophy about life — that any kind of talent or potential can be developed to be of a high relevance to one's world.

As bad as it sounded that Tayo performed very poorly in school, it does not mean he did not have an exceptional or genius capability. How else did he become very successful without a genius ability? They termed him a dullard because he wasn't doing well in school but they failed to realize that academic ingenuity is just one of many. The ridicule they

Genius Ability Without Work is Useless

put him through in school along with his drive to prove them wrong helped Tayo discover his genius, and pushed him beyond his society-imposed limits till he made something extraordinary out of his ability. He became so good that no one could ignore him. He pushed himself extremely hard and rose above academic expectations. Tayo was not an academic genius, but he was a person who discovered his genius through hard work. Do not let the society condemn you by telling you that you are good for nothing because you are finding it hard to conform to their standard indicators of successful future. The Creator is never a partial God; He gave all of us abilities that will make us amount to significance in life. It is left for everyone to discover such abilities resident within us and through diligence develop it until no one can deny that we are truly a genius.

My friend, it is not life that automatically brings shame to people; whatever you decide to do with your life will determine whether you remain a victim of ignominy or you become a victor. What would you rather be — a victim or a victor? Refuse to be an object of pity; and decide with all the strength and vigor you can possibly gather that you will add all the work needed to your genius ability to become the envy of your world.

What do you think about Tayo's mates who were academic geniuses in school? Why would their virtue of potentially great value not be so much fruitful for them in life as originally expected? The answer is simple — They discovered their genius early in school but did not work hard enough to develop it; they chose not to convert their ability to a virtue of immense value to people. Genius ability is a great virtue we are all endowed with, but not many people take maximum advantage of their capabilities. No wonder not too many people are proud of the kind of life they are living today. Working on your genius ability to develop it for the good of your world is a matter of choice; the choices you make today to work hard or to slack off at maximizing your talents determine where you find yourself tomorrow.

ACADEMIC PROWESS IS NOT SYNONYMOUS TO RICHES

Your academic prowess does not automatically translate to financial success. What will make you excel is how effectively you use your ability and how hard you work to get to the height the Creator intended for your life. The truth is — it is not just great potential that makes you relevant and rich; hard work and perseverance are almost as important as whatever ability you have. Commit yourself to hard work irrespective of the level of your discovered intellectual abilities, and watch your great potentials shine for the whole world to see.

Folorunsho Alakija is an entrepreneur and one of the richest woman in Africa. She never attended any university, yet she is far wealthier than many who did. Mrs. Alakija went to a fashion school and after years of hard work, she emerged as the best designer in the country. Her status as one of the best designers brought her so much wealth and influence she was able to grow her business further, she invested in the oil and gas industry and boom! in a matter of years, she became one of the wealthiest women in the world. Folorunsho didn't show many signs of intellectual genius as a child, but when she discovered her talent, she took it and used it to propel herself to the top rungs of personal achievement in life. This is a challenge to you — have people ridiculed you for being dull? You must take whatever ability you have and make good use of it, so much so, that in the end, there will be no doubting the fact that you were never dull; you only took some time to find your niche. This is also a challenge to you if you found your ability early in life; do not rest on your laurels, without hard work, people will point to you and say, "He/she was the best in our class that year, now, his/her life doesn't reflect the genius they showed when they were younger." To avoid this voice of scorn, you must strive to convert your intellectual genius to success, both personally and financially.

> *Nothing in this world can take the place of persistence. Talent will not; nothing is more common than unsuccessful men with talent. Genius will not; unrewarded genius is almost a proverb. Education will not; the world is full of educated derelicts. Persistence and determination alone are omnipotent.*
> CALVIN COOLIDGE

Many people think that people with exceptionally high IQ will be the richest and the most successful in the world. They think those that graduate with the best grades will go on to live awesome lives with millions in their bank accounts and lots of accomplishments. This should be the case but it will never happen without hard work. Just like Calvin Coolidge said in the quotation above, the world is filled with people that are known to be very intelligent but they are currently living an almost irrelevant life. Most people have thought that education in the formal school system is what will give them relevance in life, but this is not true — neither education nor talent will take the place of diligence and hard work. Many people have died penniless and broke because all they were on earth were nothing more than educated derelict. They never really understood the importance of smart diligence and hard work as a non-negotiable requirement in bringing oneself to the lime light. Insignificance and disappointments about life is the fate of people who rely on their genius alone, people who felt that all they needed to succeed was just their intellectual ability without seeing the place of hard work. I urge you not to repeat their mistakes; if you don't combine hard work with your genius ability, the result is a life lived in poverty or trapped in the rat race of mindlessly working for salary; a life without hard work is a life devoid of significance.

> *The only genius that's worth anything is the genius for hard work.*
> KATHLEEN WINSOR

Truth be told, the labor market is full of people running to and fro looking for jobs. The current state of the economy has made it seemingly impossible to find gainful employment, and as a result, thousands of people with good grades are unable to find jobs. Not long ago, the Federal Inland Revenue Service (FIRS) in Nigeria opened their portal to applicants; they had 500 slots and they invited people to apply for an opportunity to work with them. To their surprise, over 700, 000 applicants applied; out of this lot, over 2,000 graduated with first class degrees. The folks at FIRS couldn't believe it, almost a million unemployed graduates applied for 500 slots, and out of them, more than 2000 had the highest university grade attainable. Can you imagine? Thousands of intellectual geniuses sitting at home, jobless. This is not too far from what happens in many countries around the world, and it goes to prove to you that being eminent in life is not just about your genius capability. It is very much possible to know that you have a genius capability and still be useless and irrelevant. Making yourself useful and relevant on this earth has more to do with the hard work that you add to your talent to create value that everyone is looking for. What is the essence of your genius capability if it will not be converted to something of immense value and significance to your community, your nation and the world at large? It is not the potential you have inside of you that guarantees your relevance on this earth, it is the work you do to convert your potentials into highly useful and needful products and services that determines your place and your financial net worth in the society.

Recently, a first class graduate of mathematics from the University of Benin went on twitter to share his bitter experience. Abiola Babatunde Lasisi stated that he graduated in 2014 and since then, he has been unable to secure a job. He desperately cried out for help and employment. And to show how serious he was, he even shared his certificate online as a proof. This is the same manner many graduates with exceptional academic records have been languishing in the sorrow of joblessness. This is not the way it should be; minds like these are meant to be creating jobs instead of looking for jobs. How unpleasant it is to see great minds not knowing the role of hard and smart work in delivering the glorious destiny their amazing talents have promised.

Another example is one I came across on nairaland.com — A first class graduate opened a thread titled *"Pains of a first class graduate in Nigeria."* He was also an unemployed first class graduate who felt dejected, and he started the thread to see if there were others like him. He said, *"Sometimes, I wish I'd made a comfortable second class upper or even lower. If I'd made a second class upper or lower like most other people did, nobody would expect me to have the answer to every question, simply because I'm a first class graduate."* Clearly, the people's expectation of him was too high for him to achieve.

These examples above are geniuses. Why are they not wealthy or living a significant life? Why are they still in the labor market competing with others who graduated with average results? Face the fact — Genius ability does not automatically translate to wealth or significance. You cannot be a genius and expect wealth to fall into your laps unless you work to create it.

Do you know the difference between you and the person who is acknowledged as a genius? Your differences are in your desires, drive, and determination. Success — financial or not — takes hard work and channeling your mental resources in the right direction. How much do you want to be exceptional in life in terms of creativity and inventiveness? How much do you want to develop your genius ability? How much do you want to take advantage of your unique potentials? The level to which you want to see yourself shine forth determines how well you put work into discovering and developing the great and precious talents the Creator has put within you.

DISCOVER THE GREAT TREASURE IN YOU THROUGH WORK

> *So the Lord God took the man [He had made] and settled him in the Garden of Eden to cultivate and keep it.*
> GENESIS 2 V 15

> *So the Lord God formed out of the ground every animal of the field and every bird of the air, and brought them to Adam to see what he would call them; and whatever the man called a living creature, that was its name. And the man gave names to all the livestock, and to the birds of the air, and to every animal of the field...*
> GENESIS 2 V 19-20

The first man ever created, Adam, was inbuilt with a lot of potentials and he didn't have any idea those abilities were in him. But the Creator came up with the greatest invention for him to discover every hidden treasure within him, and to be able to utilize them to fulfill the glorious plan and destiny that He had prepared for man. This greatest invention of the Creator for mankind was WORK.

Friend, I want to tell you that one of the best things that can ever happen to you is to discover the treasure and the remarkable benefits of work. And do not make a mistake: your work is not your job; your work is what you were created to do on earth while your job is what you do to make a living on this earth. Your work simply means doing everything necessary to provide solutions to the problems you were born to solve while your job is conversion of your skills and energy for monetary rewards. It is through work that you will find out that you are not an ordinary person, not necessarily through your job; it is through work that you will discover that there is an unusual form of greatness within you which is awaiting manifestation; and definitely, it is through work that you will convert all your precious potentials into an uncommon significance and an undeniable relevance for your world.

Before the Creator gave man anything else, the first thing He gave man was work. He settled man in the Garden of Eden to cultivate and keep it. The Creator would not have told man to work if He had not already put what it takes to do the work inside of man. He wanted man to produce the best of products out of that land called Eden; He knew that the more man worked, the greater the capacity to discover greater things about the wonderful investment He had put into man. In the same vein, if you do not start actively doing the work that the Creator has called you to do, you can only discover very little about the great and amazing potentials that are resident within you. The more work you do, the more an amazement you become to yourself and to your world.

Who could have imagined that a single man can develop a naming system for billions of species of animals and birds of the air? Every kind of animal and bird that is on the surface of the earth today was brought to Adam, and he had the intellectual capacity to give names to all of them without running into confusion. It takes only genius capability to do this kind of feat. And there is no way to access the great genius capability within you without accepting to do the work that you were born to do.

In case you don't know, this world is full of problems and challenges, just as it was with Adam in the Garden of Eden when one of his first monumental challenges was to give names to all creatures found on earth. But he was able to conquer that challenge and solve that problem through the use of the great genius capability within him which was discovered through work. Everybody on this earth today is here to solve at least, a certain problem; every calling and destiny is always about filling a gap and meeting a certain need. If you do not understand and accept to solve the problems you were born to solve, you have a limited chance of knowing or realizing the extent and magnitude of the great treasure that is buried within you. You were not created to be a nonentity or be useless in life. It is only through the invention of work that you discover and develop your genius capabilities to become relevant to your world.

NO RAIN WHEN THERE IS NO MAN TO WORK

And every plant of the field before it was in the earth, and every herb of the field before it grew: for the Lord God had not caused it to rain upon the earth, and there was not a man to till the ground.
GENESIS 2 V 5

In the verse of scripture above, it is easy to discover that the reason why God did not send rain to the earth was because there was no man. And it was not just because there was no man, there was no man to work. Rain only began to pour on the earth after God created man, put him in the Garden of Eden and gave him the instruction to work. It was not until after man had taken responsibility to till the earth, to develop the earth and to nurture it that God let the rain fall. When man was now available and willing to work on earth, God began to pour the rain and things began to happen.

Until somebody was now available to take responsibility to replenish the earth; until someone was ready to work, and not just to work, but to work hard on the earth, there was no rain on the earth. We are all awaiting the rain of prosperity and abundance in our nation. We are all awaiting the rain of national development. But God will not send any rain upon us until we are ready and willing to begin to do the right kind of work. Until we all accept individual and personal responsibility, the development of our nation that we earnestly crave and desire will continue to be a mirage.

I am a pastor but I know that being a pastor does not mean I am only restricted to preaching and teaching in the church. Being a pastor does not mean I can utilize my genius capability. And I know that the only way to manifest one's genius is through hard work. I want to let you know that I am a Pastor but I personally discovered a technology I could use to make myself relevant on social media. By myself, I figured out how to maximize my influence on Facebook and on other social media platforms. It happened that I was writing a book and my publisher in America told me that we needed to extend and expand my Facebook reach. That was because I was having just fifty thousand followers as at that time. The publisher told me he had some specialists who work on Facebook publicity. He told me they can easily build a large followership on Facebook. So, they brought me the proposal; and when I looked at it, I was disappointed to see that they were claiming they could give me three hundred new 'likes' every month and they wanted me to pay $700 for that service every month. I told them that I was already having five hundred new likes every week all by myself, without spending money. Then I thought to myself that I could discover how to use social media. Last year, I was having fifty thousand followers and now I am already having half a million. With my discovery, now I am able to add one hundred thousand new followers every month. And besides that, my Facebook page has at least eight percent of the total reach Facebook is having. I came up with the technology that achieved this purpose. This is to let you know that you can achieve anything via hard work. The genius ability in you would just be laying in dormancy and waste if you are not using it and developing it.

Can you imagine people like the Wright brothers who had so much genius in them; imagine they did not work hard to fulfil their potential! They were not even engineers they were just miners and later became bicycle repairers, yet they discovered the technology of flying and are still till today known as the inventors of airplanes. There are people who studied engineering in the university for six years and have not been able to discover anything in the world of engineering. Let me shock you — I just came up with a discovery which is going to be better than Mark Zuckerberg's invention of Facebook. We now live in a civilized world, where your genius ability can shine more easily. Now is not hundred years ago where there was no technology; there is now a lot of information available for free, especially on the internet if you are ready to work hard; it is now much more possible than ever to become a star in the area of your passion or desire. The only way to escape a useless life is by being dedicated to hard work.

I am sure that you have been able to see from this chapter that without adding tremendous hard work to your genius capability, you may just be living a useless life. You must have understood that you will not be able to imagine how great and capable the talents and potentials you have within you until you become responsible enough to start working towards the fulfilment of your destiny by solving the problems you were born to solve. In the next chapter, I will be showing you how the discovery and the development of your genius capability can contribute immensely to the development of your nation.

GOLDEN NUGGETS
FROM CHAPTER 2

1. The Creator is never a partial God; He gave all of us abilities that will make us amount to significance in life. It is left for everyone to discover such abilities resident within us and through diligence develop it until no one can deny that we are truly a genius.

2. It is not life that automatically brings shame to people; whatever you decide to do with your life will determine whether you remain a victim of ignominy or you become a victor.

3. Working on your genius ability to develop it for the good of your world is a matter of choice; the choices you make today to work hard or to slack off at maximizing your talents determine where you find yourself tomorrow.

4. Your academic prowess does not automatically translate to financial success. What will make you excel is how effectively you use your ability and how hard you work to get to the height the Creator intended for your life.

5. It is not just great potential that makes relevant and wealthy; hard work and perseverance are almost as important as whatever ability you have. Commit yourself to hard work irrespective of the level of your discovered intellectual abilities, and watch your great potentials shine for the whole world to see.

6. Making yourself useful and relevant on this earth has a lot to do with the hard work that you add to your talent to create value that everyone is looking for.

7. It is not the potential you have inside of you that guarantees your relevance on this earth, it is the work you do to convert your potentials into highly useful and needful products and services that determines your place and your financial net worth in the society.

8. Genius ability does not automatically translate to wealth or significance. You cannot be a genius and expect wealth to fall into your laps unless you work to create it.

9. The level to which you want to see yourself shine forth determines how well you put work into discovering and developing the great and precious talents the Creator has put within you.

10. If you do not understand and accept to solve the problems you were born to solve, you have a limited chance of knowing or realizing the extent and magnitude of the great treasure that is buried within you.

11. You were not created to be a nonentity or be useless in life. It is only through the invention of work that you discover and develop your genius capabilities to become relevant to your world.

CHAPTER 3

DO NOT WASTE YOUR GENIUS; DEVELOP YOUR NATION

Sometimes, one is tempted to think that the higher the population of a country, the easier it should be for the nation to make tremendous progress in channeling her resources to achieve some economic advancement — China, for example, is proving that there may be some element of truth in this notion. But there are other nations in Africa and Asia that are being dragged in the mud of economic stagnation due to large negligence by her citizens to productively utilize the great potentials within them.

Have you ever wondered why a country of more than 150 million people will be struggling with developing her economy or providing a better standard of living for her citizens? What could be the main reason for this? Many people will say it is corruption; others say bad governance; while some say it is the fault of the British or European colonials. Yet, ridiculously, some people attribute the development of great nations to luck; what a silly way to think! Until we all realize that the advancement of a nation comes as a result of the development of the potentials of the people of that nation by accepting their individual responsibilities, we will continue to ignorantly put the blame on other entities (like the government) that have little or nothing to do about the problem.

> *God and Nature first made us what we are,*
> *and then out of our own created genius*
> *we make ourselves what we want to be.*
> *Follow always that great law. Let the sky*
> *and God be our limit and Eternity our*
> *measurement.*
> MARCUS GARVEY

There is no other way to advance a nation apart from the use of genius capabilities. When we have a situation where only a few people in a nation have discovered their genius potentials and just a minute percentage of people are committed to developing these capabilities to a point where the nation can start benefitting from it, there will be little that can be achieved in terms of economic development and improvement in standard of living for her populace. Marcus Garvey rightly said in the quote above — no matter what nature or sequence of events has made happen to a people, they can make themselves whatever they want to be by creating their own genius and there will be no measurement on which to base the accomplishment of the people of such nation because it will be infinite and endless. People who take out time to create and build their own genius cannot be limited in life; they continue to be relevant until eternity.

A lot of people in third world nations keep complaining about corrupt governance, inflation, inadequate infrastructures, and poor educational system to mention but a few; but how many people are looking inwards to see if there are solutions within them that have not been thoroughly harnessed? How many times have we asked ourselves this question: "what is the difference between me and folks like Bill Gates, Warren Buffet, Jeff Bezos, Larry Page, Elon Musk and many others who have made giant strides in the United States and have contributed largely to the sustenance of a comparatively virile economy of their country?" It is great people that make a great nation and we all already have the seed of greatness within us. Therefore, in this chapter, I will be showing you that it takes the hard work of accepting responsibility on everybody's part to contribute our immense greatness of potentials and capabilities to the development of our dear nations. Even if the country you live is already developed, it can always get better.

DO NOT KILL YOUR GREAT POTENTIALS

Many times, when the exceptional capabilities that people are endowed with are not discovered and nurtured to the point of greatness, then such talents may not be able to escape death. This is the reason why a lot of people have suffered unduly from the untimely mortality of dreams in their hearts; and many people have regretfully gone to the grave with their great potentials inside of them. This could have been the sad case of Olabisi when the school system and even her parents did not recognize the great gifting that she was packaged with by her Creator.

"What do you want to be in future?" Olabisi remembered years ago when her school teacher asked each pupil in the class the important question, while she was teaching them how to write a composition on 'Myself'.

"I want to be a doctor!" Many little fingers were raised but the little mouths uttered the enviable profession before the teacher could permit any of them to talk. Miss Hassan nodded her approval of the profession. "Yes, it's good to be a doctor, you can work in hospitals and make good money". She looked at the pupils that have not spoken and asked them what they wanted to be. A beautiful and neatly dressed girl, Tolani, raised up her hand.

"Yes?" Miss Hassan permitted her. "I want to be a banker in future and make lots of money." The class erupted in an uproar. The teacher hit the table with her cane. "Why are you all shouting? Tolani is right. Give her a round of applause!" and the young ones obediently complied. Miss Hassan continued her counselling. "Why do you think you are all in school? Is it not to study hard so that you can have a well-paid job in the future? Your parents are struggling now to put you through school. You had better be serious about your studies so that you can take good care of them in old age."

The teacher then pointed to Olabisi…

Twenty-five years later, still fresh in her memory as if it happened yesterday, she remembered her fear when the teacher suddenly called her. All along she had been busy trying to draw beautiful Miss Hassan as she faced the board. Bisi quickly slipped her drawing sheet to the floor when she saw teacher pointing at her.

"Olabisi! What about you?" The girl quickly dropped her paper and tried hiding her pencil. She struggled to her feet, slightly shivering.

"Art, Draw. I want to be a drawer in future", the little girl stammered her reply.

Another round of laughter erupted in the class. But the laughter went down and became smiles and murmurs as the teacher rebuked them. The teacher drew closer to Bisi and said, "Did you mean to say you want to become an artist in future? People who draw are called artists. But Bisi, artists don't make money. Is it not somebody who has filled his stomach, wardrobe and bank account that will think of paying somebody to draw him?" Afterwards, she decided to punish her for engaging in drawing activities when she was supposed to be paying attention to her.

Olabisi obeyed her teacher, she stopped drawing in school but she kept drawing at home. She wanted to study Fine Arts in a Polytechnic but her parents would have none of it. Her father insisted that she must study law in a university in order to secure her future. She went on to study Law, and her parents celebrated her success and were ready to send her to Law school. That was when the reality hit her. She realized she had to make her choice: either go to Law school to make her parents happy and herself frustrated for life, or she could try and convince her parents one more time and go for the love of her life, Creative Arts.

She drew a portrait of her mother and gave her as a gift on Mothers' day. While her mother was admiring the artwork, Olabisi went on her knees and pleaded with her mother. She requested that her mother help persuade her father on the issue. Bisi went ahead and wrote an undertaking, committing herself to succeed on the field within the next five years. She signed her own part and begged her parents with tears, to sign their portions. Her parents reluctantly signed it. Olabisi framed the document and placed it on the reading table in her room, for a constant reminder.

She enrolled for Fine Arts in an institution and spent her free time taking private lessons with a local portrait painter to learn the selling and business aspects of the profession. She worked hard in school, and equipped with her prior computer literacy, she excelled in school. Bisi spent every moment drawing. Towards her graduation, she applied to a book publishing house to draw for children's books. They requested samples and she presented about ten pieces. Olabisi got the freelance job. Her goal was to have her own gallery, which she achieved a year after graduating from Arts school. Now, Bisi is progressively moving towards her goal of becoming one of the best artists in the world. She has a vision of having her portraits done so excellently that at least one will be in every home in Nigeria. Is this not how we are all supposed to be developing our unique gifting and keep working towards making it the best and producing the best and the most competitive products and services in the world? This is the kind of value we should all be adding to ourselves; consistently growing our abilities towards the fulfilment of our destiny, and always striving to be the best in everything we lay our hands to do according to the calling of our Creator upon our lives. There is no other way to cause the flourishing of the great and amazing potentials inside all of us apart from focusing on our calling and not going to school or working because we want to make money. If everybody is deciding the choice of career based on how lucrative the path is, then there is little hope for that person to be useful for the development of that nation.

It is high time the purpose of education is redefined in every country. Education is supposed to be an instrument of solving the problems of the country and making the world a better place for everybody. Education should *not* be a tool for securing high paying jobs; it should be a device for fulfilling destiny. Are we to blame children who want to fulfill the desires of their parents by studying a course suggested to them? Parents should not be deciding professions for their children based on their financial status. The choice of career for every child should be based on the kind of gifts, talents, and potentials that God has put in them.

> *Everyone is born a genius, but the process of living de-geniuses them.*
> R. BUCKMINSTER FULLER

It is so unfortunate that the present value system in most countries makes it seem that until you can secure a white collar job, you cannot be successful. And this has led to the untimely death of the genius ability in people who were born as geniuses; the quote by Buckminster Fuller asserts this fact in insinuating that the process of trying to make a living has made these individuals start looking like people with no special endowments. Virtually nobody has the orientation of schooling to solve the problems of humanity in our country and continent; nearly everyone is thinking about lucrative jobs and fat salaries. Why don't we think about going to school for creating as many jobs as possible upon graduation? A man cannot live beyond what is in his thinking or imagination. If there are more people looking for jobs compared to the people creating jobs, how do we expect to even have enough jobs available for everyone?

Though you may work at a job for some time, but be fully aware that you were created to be a job creator through your innovations and inventions. But you will not practically realize your creative capabilities until you begin to work and learn for the right purpose.

How great would it be if our medical students and practitioners aim at eradicating malaria and typhoid fever in Nigeria? How awesome would it be when we get to a state in which contacting malaria is actually a miracle like it is in some developed countries? What if our medical students and researchers accept a challenge of discovering the cure for cancer before any other country? If we have been waiting and just hoping on God to make our long desired transformation happen to us one day, then we may keep waiting indefinitely. Let us stop deceiving ourselves and living in delusion. The surest way for us to enjoy a lasting national transformation and development is if our students and professionals discover the genius in them and they work hard to develop it and they start using it to solve the problems of the country.

But the sad story is that virtually everybody is busy working for money, and the predominant mindset for most people is the survival mentality. What about our Economics and Political Science professionals? How great would it be if their aim of going to school is to solve the problem of poverty and economic disaster in the country? The undesirable situation we have is that most of these professionals are trying to make a living and simply survive; then everyone else is trying to make a decent income that will make them revered in the society. Do not live in illusion — If survival or superiority show is the sole purpose of your existence, the genius ability within you will never shine forth.

WRONG ORIENTATION AND VALUE SYSTEM UNDERMINES NATIONAL DEVELOPMENT

As human beings, we have a lot of great potentials resident in us; but if we have the wrong orientation about life and the purpose of education, these genius aptitudes within us will remain dormant. Without sufficient hard work and commitment, majority of people will not discover the exceptional capabilities within them, not to talk of developing them. Then, how do we expect the Nation to develop? We will continue to hope and wish for economic growth and development without seeing any change if we do not all arise to the necessity of discovering the special abilities we have been endowed with from above, and make up our minds to develop these gifts and talents until they can solve the present and the long-lasting problems of our communities and our nation.

A patient once recounted what she heard from a doctor in University Teaching Hospital (UCH), Ibadan, in 2010 when she went for treatment. The doctor said, *"the tragedy of Nigeria is that our best brains are in the medical field."* He faced his students, which were present while he was examining the patient and said, *"Medical profession is for the average student. You can easily read and understand it. You can cram terminologies, diseases, and drugs. You are even free to contact a book at any point in time. Anybody can be a medical doctor. Students with great brains should be in other fields as well. They should be scientists and engineers, making breakthrough discoveries and inventions that will solve our problems. They should be economists, thinking out a solution to our money problems and curb inflation. It is a pity."*

I believe this elderly doctor is right to some extent. Some people manage to discover the special abilities within them. But it is an obvious fact that most Geniuses who discover themselves in most parts of Africa only think of getting the best jobs within and outside the country. Few people cultivate a mindset of solving the problems of their society from a young age. This is unlike some of our counterparts from the developed nations. Consider Bill Gates, who was obsessed with solving the problem of the Computer industry in his country and the world at large, right from a young age when he discovered his ability. This man had to drop out from the so called education system when he realized it was slowing him down. He was not thinking about lucrative jobs or else he would have been in bondage of the school system, and probably be running the rat race of job hunting till now. It was good old hard work that helped Gates. He refused to let societal and family influence negatively affect his discovery and the development of his Genius ability.

The mentality of the renowned Facebook founder, Mark Zuckerberg is worth considering. He visited Nigeria in 2016 and many people could not help but wonder why he visited Nigeria, of all countries in Africa. In Mark's own words, he said, *"this trip has really blown me away by the talents of young entrepreneurs and developers in this country, and making a difference and making a change. It reminds me of when I wanted to start Facebook. I wasn't starting a company at the time but wanted to build something to see if it would work. And that is what I see people here do, pushing through challenges, building things that you want to see in the world. You are not just going to change Nigeria and the whole of Africa but the whole world."* This were his words at Co-creation Hub in Yaba, Lagos, Nigeria's first open living lab and pre-incubation space, designed to be a multi-functional, multi-purpose space, where people work to catalyze creative social tech ventures. Thank goodness for places like this, a beacon of hope for Nigerian technology. If most people are working hard to discover and develop the amazing abilities in them like these people at Co-creation Hub, imagine what the situation of our country would have been like today!

Mark Zuckerberg discovered himself when he was 12 years of age. He became what he is today through sheer hard work. He made many little inventions before Facebook, which his father's dentist clinic benefitted from. This guy did not depend on anybody but on the genius potential within him to achieve success. He knew what he wanted and knew that he had what it takes inside of him.

I like to ask you this — do you know that you already have everything it takes to succeed in life inside of you? If not, you have been deceived by the ephemeral things of life. Your focus might have been diverted away from some of the most important things of life. If you have been paying attention to the things that are most crucial to your destiny — the abilities, talents, and gifting that the Creator has put inside of you, it will be difficult for you to be looking for success in other places apart from the intangible (but highly important) resources you readily have available within you. These resources deserve the most of your commitment to develop, multiply, refine and improve them especially for the benefit of humanity.

Zuckerberg initially created Facebook to serve as the regular yearbook for his faculty in school — he did not despise his genius capability; at least he tried to use it to do something. Then he discovered he could use it for something bigger — this is how this potential grew to the point that it has produced a gigantic company with humongous influence. Now, it has become a household name all over the world. As at June 2016, Facebook has 1.71 billion users, out of which 1.31 billion users are very active, they log in on daily basis. This same social media has 4.5 billion likes. Genius is definitely a desirable quality but it does not automatically translate to the development of a nation, if not coupled with an above-average diligence.

> *Conceit spoils the finest genius. There is not much danger that real talent or goodness will be overlooked long; even if it is, the consciousness of possessing and using it well should satisfy one, and the great charm of all power is modesty.*
> LOUISA MAY ALCOTT

Because of the infective money-conscious orientation that is prevalent in many African countries, brain drain has become another ugly monster largely depriving Africa the contribution of her geniuses. As correctly said by Louisa in the quote above, self-conceit, pride of life, and lust of the eyes are some of the major reasons for the spoiling of many people's geniuses. They continue to live in the great danger of overlooking their talents and abilities and they never come to true satisfaction because they do not live in modesty that will allow the power of their genius shine forth.

Over ninety percent of first class students graduating from Nigerian universities find and use every means to travel abroad to different developed countries around the world. They claim to have a genuine excuse for going there to further their studies but most of them never go back home to cause a transformation of their nation with the acquired knowledge. Most people are so much concerned about survival and trying to live a 'better' life that they have made it the sole purpose of their existence. There are verifiable rumours that a large percentage of outstanding medical doctors based in the United States are Nigerians. These are people with amazing potentials and capabilities that could put heads together to solve scores of problems afflicting their dear nation.

The present value system is the one that makes many graduates aspire to work for top companies like Shell, Chevron, Total, or any oil company in a bid to just be wealthy at the detriment of the discovery of the genius capabilities that is capable of bringing them true greatness; the Maths geniuses want to work in banks rather than making mathematical discoveries that will lead to breakthroughs in several industries in the country. Until the value system in the nation changes to that of hard work and personal responsibility consciousness, genius potentials will continue to waste in people and the economic development of the nation will remain continuously and unnecessarily challenged.

The Creative and Innovative Power of a Genius

> *Any intelligent fool can make things bigger and more complex... It takes a touch of genius — and a lot of courage to move in the opposite direction.*
>
> E. F. SCHUMACHER

We have a lot of professors with exceptional talents in this country but it is not showing in any significant contribution to national development. Undergraduates are mandated to carry out practical projects in School before graduation; this part of the curriculum was put there to ignite the flash of genius in the upcoming professionals. But these graduate research projects have largely become redundant activities in most universities. About ninety-five percent of such genuinely carried out projects are abandoned for one reason or the other. The truth in the quote by Schumacher above may be bitter, but it needs to be heeded. What a lot of intelligent people in our country do is to make things more complicated and eventually abandoned. The true touch of the genius ability within us is to solve problems and make life easier for as many people as possible through the force of courage and hard work.

In science programmes on television, we see such mini-projects demonstrated, eco-friendly cars, water-fuelled generators, model aeroplanes and many more. Many of these efforts by young people do not get to a point where they get produced on a massive scale to benefit the whole country. Most of the times, the geniuses responsible for such witty demonstrations get their purpose diverted in the search for money to better fit in the society or in the guise of not having enough capital for mass production. It is important to note that the best form of capital you can have is your genius capability but it will not be of much use to the nation if hard work is not applied to make the seemingly impossible become possible.

HARDSHIP SHOULD AWAKEN YOUR GENIUS; NOT TO KILL IT

One of the best persons to learn the lesson of responsibility and gain a proper orientation from is William Kamkwamba, a Malawian innovator, engineer, and author. He gained fame in his country when, in 2002, he built a wind turbine to power a few electrical appliances in his family's house in Wimbe using blue gum trees, bicycle parts, and materials collected in a local scrapyard. Since then, he has built a solar-powered water pump that supplies the first drinking water in his village and two other wind turbines (the tallest of which is standing at 12 meters (39 ft)). He is planning to build two more, including one in Lilongwe, the political capital of Malawi. He was not complaining about lack of capital; he understood that the power of genius capability is to provide solutions irrespective of the limiting factors and situations that may be showing their ugly faces around.

> *Genius is independent of situation.*
> CHARLES CHURCHILL

Wow! This young man is amazing. He solved at least a problem for his community. Instead of joining others to keep complaining about the economic hardship and recession in your country, why don't you do something to solve a little problem? The situation you are going through may not

THE CREATIVE AND INNOVATIVE POWER OF A GENIUS

be as worse as what Kamkwamba was passing through before he came up with his wonderful inventions. As Charles Churchill correctly said in the quote above, the genius ability within you is not dependent on or affected by the situation on the outside; no matter what happens around you, your potential remains the same until you begin to take conscious efforts to build it and utilize it to turn the situation of things around.

A crippling famine forced Kamkwamba to drop out of school, and he was not able to return to school because his family was unable to afford the tuition fee. In a desperate attempt to retain his education, Kamkwamba began to frequently visit the school library. It was there that Kamkwamba discovered his true love and incredible genius for electronics. Before, he had once set up a small business repairing his village's radios, but his work with the radios had not earned much money. This was not just enough to stop him; he would not be part of those people saying the government or famine or economic recession is the reason for their misfortune in life. He knew he had the abilities within him to be a solution to the problems confronting his people; and he worked extremely hard to convert his discovered genius potential into a life of significance, in spite of the pervasive famine and hardship that would have killed the dreams of many others. You do not have any excuse not to make yourself relevant in your nation; all you need is to discover what you have, and begin to grow it until you practically become a saviour to others by solving the problems that are threatening their God-given lives.

Kamkwamba, after reading a book called "Using Energy", decided to create a makeshift wind turbine. He experimented with a small model using a cheap dynamo and eventually made a functioning wind turbine that powered some electrical appliances in his family's house. Local farmers and journalists investigated the spinning device and Kamkwamba's fame in international news skyrocketed.

Friend, you need to know that there is nothing like productively utilizing your genius ability; this is because the more you use it, the more you discover something else you can do with it. The more you work with your genius potentials, the better you can resolve the problems plaguing your nation and you will be able to put smiles on the faces of many people. Imagine everybody contributing and solving one or two problems here and there using their specific talents and special gifting, the story would not have been what it is today in our dear country.

The essence of this book is to open your eyes to see that you already have great potentials inside of you that can bless your Nation and your world, and it will be a great shame on you and a disservice to humanity if you choose not to find out your exceptional capabilities. It will be a time of regret and sorrow for you when you meet your Creator before you realize that you have wasted all the wonderful treasures He has invested in you. Without knowing the true meaning of work, a Nation may be full of geniuses but will have virtually nothing to show for it.

In this chapter, you have learnt that genius discovery and development is one of the most crucial factors responsible for national development in any country. All the advancement of developed nations we see today is as a result of responsibility consciousness of many of their citizens.

If any nation is going to truly experience a lasting transformation, it is extremely important that the people of that nation re-configure their value system in such a way that it appreciates the discovery of individual genius capabilities and devotes attention to the development of people with such potentials into indisputable problem solvers. In the next chapter, you will be learning how to make sure you are not abusing the genius ability you already have but rather be investing it.

GOLDEN NUGGETS FROM CHAPTER 3

1. Until we all realize that the advancement of a nation comes as a result of the development of the potentials of the people of that nation by accepting their individual responsibilities, we will continue to ignorantly put the blame on other entities (like the government) that have little or nothing to do about the problem.

2. People who take out time to create and build their own genius cannot be limited in life; they continue to be relevant until eternity.

3. There is no other way to cause the flourishing of the great and amazing potentials inside all of us apart from focusing on our calling. It doesn't come by living for money.

4. Education is supposed to be an instrument of solving the problems of the country and making the world a better place for everybody. Education should not be a tool for securing high paying jobs; it should be a device for fulfilling destiny.

5. Though you may work at a job for some time, but be fully aware that you were created to be a job creator through your innovations and inventions. But you will not practically realize

your creative capabilities until you begin to
work and learn for the right purpose.

6. We will continue to hope and wish for economic growth and development without seeing any change if we do not all arise to the necessity of discovering the special abilities we have been endowed with from above, and make up our minds to develop these gifts and talents until they can solve the present and the long-lasting problems of our communities and our nation.

7. Until the value system in the nation changes to that of hard work and personal responsibility consciousness, genius potentials will continue to waste in people and the economic development of the nation will remain continuously and unnecessarily challenged.

8. The true touch of the genius ability within us is to solve problems and make life easier for as many people as possible through the force of courage and hard work.

9. You do not have any excuse not to make yourself relevant in your nation; all you need is to discover what you have, and begin to grow it until you practically become a saviour to others by solving the problems that are threatening their God-given lives.

10. The more you work with your genius potentials, the better you can resolve the problems plaguing your nation and you will be able to put smiles on the faces of many people.

11. Without knowing the true meaning of work,
a Nation may be full of geniuses but will
have virtually nothing to show for it.

# CHAPTER 4

DO NOT ABUSE YOUR GENIUS; INVEST IT

If you have been following my line of discussion so far, you would have realized the great importance of genius ability to ourselves, to people around us, to the Nation and to the world at large. But something in particular that is note-worthy is that a number of people who have actually discovered and are convinced that they have exceptional abilities in certain areas have simply been abusing it.

This may not certainly be your case but you need to ask yourself the following question — *"What is that thing that I know how to do better than anyone else around me that I have not been using positively?"* Without assumptions, pondering on this question thoroughly may help you identify even some of your genius abilities that you have not realized or those you have been unconsciously using for unworthy causes.

> *When the purpose of a thing is not known, abuse is inevitable.*
> MYLES MUNROE

For instance, quite a number of people are very good talkers who can command a lot of attention but what they use their gift to do is to run people down; a capability that could have been used to influence a huge number of people positively. Some of the best brains in our country today are into armed robbery because they could not secure jobs, even after a couple of years upon graduation — then, they become a prey and easily influenced by bad gangs. They have lost the purpose of their genius ability and instead, they are abusing what should have been a great investment for them and for their nations.

The irony of life is that when we hear of criminals (like notorious robbers and unforgiving terrorists) who are doing evil things in our society, much of our focus is on the corrupt and wicked things they do. Only a little attention is paid to the fact that many of these people are actually achieving these malicious deeds through their God-given genius abilities. Sometimes, the worst of all men is the one with the best ever seen potential. Oh how I wish everyone's eyes, who is using his ability negatively in Africa and all around the world become opened to the fact that he or she can achieve an unimaginable level of greatness if these capabilities are channeled in the right direction; how I wish that we all absolutely realize that wasted energy and abused potentials cause more unnecessary problems in this world than we ever imagine. It is never too late because you can still make a U-turn from the way of destruction that ends in great pain. As we ride on along this journey of discovering and developing your genius capabilities, I will like you to learn a few lessons from the stories of some of the brightest minds in our country as would be related in this chapter.

THE STORY OF SEGUN, THE GENIUS

I've known people with exceptional talent — and some have wasted it...
GEOFFREY BOYCOTT

It was indeed a bad day for Segun and his cohorts — "*Let the people present Exhibit D,*" the prosecutor announced as 2 men rolled a TV unit into the courtroom. The TV set flickered on, and Segun, the defendant, almost jumped out of his chair when he saw what the judge was about to watch; he had no doubt he was doomed.

For the next 15 minutes, the Judge watched spellbound as a group of 4 men gathered close to the vault of The People's Merchant Bank. Three of them were focused on the fourth man, the defendant, Segun. They watched in awe as he went to work on the lock combination; a high security dual control combination lock. Normally, the bank vault shouldn't open unless 2 security keys are inserted concurrently, along with the thumbprint of the Bank Manager and two other employees, but Segun was the best vault-breaker in the country, if not the whole of Africa and he'd cracked even more complicated locks. They were short on time, and their nerves were frayed, "Hurry up, Sege," one of the assailants said, and as if on cue, the lock combination groaned open. Segun had done it again; but now in the courtroom, he had a sheepish grin on his face and when the prosecutor paused the video, the predatory smile on his face remained frozen on the screen even as the Judge cleared his throat to speak.

"I just watched a young man break into one of the most secure vaults in the country, and what I feel is a mixture of anger, grief, and regret. Yes, regret! I don't know if you're aware, but you have a gift. You have an exceptional ability, you have a rare gift, but rather than use it to your advantage, you chose to misuse it; you chose to use it to rob people of their hard-earned money. With your ability, you could have worked for the biggest security companies in the world; in fact, you could have started your own vault-building business, employ people like you and play your part in upraising your family and your country. Instead, you're going to jail for a long time; your ability — an ability that could have helped you, your family and many other people will rot in prison with you because you chose the path of a criminal. Mr. Segun, you've abused your talent, and you'll spend the rest of your life regretting it."

Segun was sentenced to spend years of his life in prison. But do you know that the worst prison of life is not the one that criminals are put? The worst prison of life is believing that you are in a condition where your exceptional capabilities can only be expressed negatively. The worst of all incarcerations is knowing that you have genius abilities but you cannot find any way to express it according to the design of your Creator. Segun could crack open the most complicated safe combinations in the world, but he wasn't aware of the ways he could have used that ability to his advantage without breaking the law. People saw him as the smartest but at the end, he was still the most stupid.

Where has your smartness led you? Are you in the most painful crisis of your life now because what you thought was the best way to use your abilities eventually landed you in trouble? Realize that you cannot fight against the design of God — He designed this earth in such a way that, even if we have discovered our unusual and supernormal abilities, only through WORK can we be able to utilize them for maximum benefit to mankind in spite of obvious limiting challenges that seem to stop other people. Without putting in necessary work, you will not be able to overcome the overwhelming temptations of using your great potentials in the most negative ways. Hard work and persistence is what distinguishes the shining star from the hopeless criminal.

THE GENIUS OF NIGERIAN SCAMMERS

Not long ago, an article on the 'Nigeria World Blog' described in some detail some incredibly smart — though nefarious — abilities shown by the notorious Nigerian scammers, 'the yahoo boys'. These boys know their ways around many organizational requirements, and they would write fake letters with fake names, armed with a business proposal; often, an offer to transfer huge amounts of money from one endangered or unclaimed bank account to the prospective victim's account with the promise that the unsuspecting victim will be given a substantial cut of the proceeds. They would tender fake documents and photographs in the course of persuading him/her to reveal his/her private information; once the target sends them the details, all the money in the victim's account disappears.

These boys know the requirements of many banks, the banking laws in different countries, and they are very adept at writing sound business plans — all to swindle people out of their funds. Do you know that all these abilities make them qualified to work and be one of the most influential persons at some of the biggest banks around? I am sure you can guess the reason why they have given up hopes on talents that could make them become one of the greatest in their spheres of influence. It is simple, yet they keep missing it — WORK — As you have been told in the previous chapter, work is one of the most marvelous inventions of the Creator. Without it, one would be condemned to a useless and a frustrating life. The talents that were put in you by your Creator are like seeds; it takes work to develop them to the point of fruitfulness and flourishing to your world; no other short-cut can get you there.

The work that some of these boys might have needed to add to their great potentials may just have been going to school to get a degree so they can be recognized in their respective industries. But laziness and irresponsibility have killed a lot of potentials; it has contributed to a lot of untapped riches that eventually end up in the grave. My friend, please make up your mind that your story will not end on a sad note; make up your mind that you will put in all the work required to the best of your capability to maximize the genius ability that you were created with for the best of your community, your nation, and the world.

When you talk to some of these fraudsters, few of them would even say, "*I know how to hustle. I am smarter than those bankers!*" Many of them do not know that what they are taking for granted — what they abuse — is a genius business brain, an exceptional capability that could have yielded results in the order of the exploits of the biggest business moguls that can be found in the country. Through ignorance, a lot of people abuse some great potentials that could make them enlisted as some of the richest folks in the continent. Imagine how greatly the economy of our country could benefit from these fraudsters if they are using their energies, their talents, their genius potentials in the most positive way. What do you think could have been the story of our dear nation today if all these fraudsters that are caught in one criminal activity or the other, both home and abroad are making positive giant strides instead of dragging the name of our country in the mud? The image of our country far and near could have been more of glory and less of shame; many more people could have been so proud of their origin and country of birth. But I can tell you that the tables will turn if we can get everybody committed to believing in the precious gifts in them, and if they can be diligent enough to develop their potentials to the point where it can be useful for as many people as possible.

Dear reader, this is a time to also examine yourself — What gift do you have that you have been abusing? Have you been contributing to other people's lives with your talents or you are adding more to people's woes because of your selfish desires? Selfishness is a deadly bug that will never allow you maximize your potentials. You cannot keep thinking of yourself alone and expect the light of your genius ability to shine to your generation. The greatest known geniuses of all times were never selfish; they keep on thinking of how to use their abilities to bless the world. This is the same thing you need to do to make your genius ability flourish.

TWO GENIUS HACKERS

Now, let me tell you about the case of two Nigerian hackers who developed a malware and sent it as attachments to many customers of a particular bank in India; the plan was, once the victim opens the attachment, he/she has unwittingly given the hackers access to his/her email. The boys were caught after using a customer's details — gotten from his email — to dupe him out of almost $115 000. These boys showed excellent planning and execution abilities; they not only created a malware, they coordinated the attacks on people's emails and succeeded in making millions of naira off their effort.

With the abilities these boys portrayed, do you agree with me that they could have done lots of good and profitable work with their lives? Are you also of a similar opinion with me that they could have been employed and be more useful as the owner of some of the biggest software firms in the world? Instead, they were looking for a fast means that would not involve or include the kind of work that they were created to do.

The most important work you were created to do is to multiply your talents, and the only way to multiply your gifting and abilities is through positive work. If you are engaged in a negative work, it will eventually catch up with you and hamper your destiny; you cannot get anywhere far with a negative lifestyle. In case you don't know, a negative lifestyle is one that is against the design of your Creator. It is the one that makes people waste away behind bars and for example, in the case of these hackers, instead of using their abilities to take Nigeria's name far and wide for good reasons, they chose to abuse their genius ability and dragged our great country's name even lower.

I want to challenge you today to use your life as profitable as possible because I know it is not as difficult as people think. There are still a sizeable amount of people who are achieving great and positive results with their lives despite all odds that everyone else complains about in Africa. You don't have to use your genius to steal; you don't have to use your genius to make other people cry before you can laugh; your genius was designed by God to be used NOT for despicable, immoral and corrupt activities; your genius was designed to bless the lives of people around you and make this world a better place.

THE GENIUS BLOGGER

A good example of a man that exemplifies how genius ability is to be used is Bamidele Onibalusi. At age 16, Bamidele started writing for people online; he did data entry jobs, funded online surveys and every other job he could get his hands on. At this time, Bamidele didn't even have a personal computer; he does all the work at a cyber-café close to his house. Before long, he launched his own blog and he began to post as many write-ups as he could. He has an ethic of hard work, which is a non-negotiable requirement in the school of geniuses. This is the same prerequisite that many fraudulent and unscrupulous people are trying to avoid on a journey to prominence. Do you think you can get anywhere far and fulfilling in life if you are going opposite the direction you should go? True greatness will keep eluding you in life if you do not make up your mind to use your genius abilities exactly for the things they were designed to be used for.

Today, Bamidele's site attracts tens of thousands of visitors monthly and ranks as one of the most visited blogsites in the world. He also writes as a freelancer for some of the biggest sites in the world; sites like Business Insider, ReadWriteWeb, Problogger and DailyBlogTips.com and he makes tens of thousands of dollars every month from his blogsite and his writing. His main goal now is to train and encourage people to discover their writing talents; he aims to teach people how to make legal money from the internet (the same internet hundreds of thousands of people use for illicit activities).

Do you know that there are many people who are better versed writers than Bamidele? Some of the best writers in our nation are busy wasting their precious time and life on the internet, carefully writing insulting and derogatory comments and remarks on posts of people that are sharing their opinions on social media. They spend so much time abusing and replying insults, engaging in activities that will never add any value to their own lives or to anybody else. It is quite possible you are abusing your genius ability without consciously being aware of it; a deliberate and introspective appraisal of the use of your talents will help you make an informed decision.

Two years into his blogging career, Bamidele decided to do even better. He opened a Facebook group, and using this medium, he tutored over 100 members of his group on how to be better writers, and all 100 of them made over $2 000 within a month of receiving Bamidele's tutoring. He helped these people put better food on their table, money in their pockets; he helped them afford clothes, cars, and so on. In his own way, he enriched the nation's economy, while at the same time, mentoring budding geniuses like himself. Bamidele did not have a computer as a self-starter teenager but he did not use that as an excuse for him to abuse his discovered genius by joining internet fraudsters to perpetrate crimes in the name of bad economic situation of the country. He persisted till he made his genius shine beyond doubt. A young man in his early twenties has used his ability to help more people in 5 years than some corrupt leaders have done all their lives.

Can you now see that it is vital that after recognizing your genius, you should go to work at utilizing it maximally; using it for good and for the betterment of your immediate environment? Bamidele did not only make himself a wealthy young man, he also helped other people realize their genius ability too. Always take note of this — an ability or talent that you are despising or abusing is the same one someone else has believed in, and has committed to achieve great accomplishments with. Which path will you take? Will you start maximizing all the potentials within you for the advancement of not only your life, but our country as a whole, or you want to continue wasting your precious gifts and endowments? You know the choice is indeed yours!

> *The saddest thing in life is wasted talent and the choices you make will shape your life forever.*
> CHAZZ PALMINTERI

As Chazz Palminteri rightly said, apart from being the saddest thing in life, you will also have to be one of the major victims if you are making a bad choices in the use of your talent; your best bet should be continual discovery, development, and positive utilization of the amazing potentials and abilities you were packaged with by the Creator.

THE BOKO HARAM GENIUS

The Boko Haram sect has been a thorn in the flesh of Nigerians and the Nigerian Military for some years now. They have laid waste to villages, killing people in the thousands, burning and bombing all in their way. It may be hard to believe because of the evil they wrought, but many of the Boko Haram insurgents are people with unbelievable genius ability; they have some of the best local bomb-makers in the country, they have excellent doctors who take care of their wounded soldiers, and a host of other personnels who contribute in one way or the other to the menace called the Boko Haram. Has it ever occurred to you that these are people with special ability, strong enough to improve our country's military? These people could have been using their endowments for the advancement of Nigeria; instead, they choose to use their God-given ability to cause destruction of human lives and property.

Well, do not be quick to judge them. All you need to do is to focus on the great treasures that God has put in humans. Think about this — how can people that are thought to be uneducated, people who are considered to be unlearned, folks that are regarded to be primitive and crude be exhibiting so much genius capability in doing evil? The answer is simple; it is an attestation to the fact that there is a great latent genius capability in everyone, it only needs an unusual level of commitment and dedication to WORK in order to reveal the genius we are created with.

The Nigerian government has sought help from many of the best anti-terrorist bodies in the world — the CIA, Interpol, and the likes — but none of them have had any success in defeating the Boko Haram. They — the Boko Haram — got many of their weapons by raiding military strongholds; showing resourcefulness that puts the Nigerian military to shame. They have groups for different purposes; some specialize in bombings, some in raiding towns and villages for food, some rob banks — and the homes of wealthy people — and others are trained to engage whomever the government sends to confront them. To have survived for more than 7 years shows how ingenious the Boko Haram are; they alternate their maneuvers frequently, and they always manage to stay a step ahead of their pursuers. Even though the military has killed thousands of them, they show no signs of easing-up. Hard as it may be to admit it, they have some impressive abilities, abilities that they not only use for the wrong purposes but also get exposed to untimely death by their actions.

Now, do not misunderstand me; I am not praising the evil ways of Boko Haram. I am only pointing your attention to the fact that everybody, including the people referred to as nonentities have genius capabilities, but it is only through WORK that everyone discovers his or her ingenuity. It is quite possible to waste an enormously prodigious potential on the wrong purpose. If these people can achieve so much evil with not so much of civilization, and not the best of technologies, imagine what they will be capable of doing if they have an education compared to the guys that work for the American CIA. They believe they're fighting "God's" battle when what they are really doing is wasting and abusing their God-given genius ability.

Do an inventory analysis of your potentials and talents. Are you utilizing them positively or abusing them? Have you been making other people cry with your shrewdness? Or you have been making people smile with your distinctive capabilities? By now, you know the path that will lead you into maximizing your genius potential — It is the path of love for humanity in dedicated work.

TEDO, THE GENIUS WOMANIZER

He who knows not and knows not he
knows not, he is a fool — shun him;
He who knows not and knows he
knows not, he is simple — teach him;
He who knows and knows not he
knows, he is asleep — wake him;
He who knows and knows he knows,
he is wise — follow him!
ARABIAN PROVERB

There is a story of a guy called Tedo who did not know who he was. He was in the category of the person that knows but does not know that he knows — he was so deep in his slumber, and yet he thought he was living life in the best way ever. You cannot be so deep in your sleep and expect your genius ability to manifest. Just as the Arabian proverb above says, you need to wake up and realize who you really are.

Tedo was a very charismatic young man and everybody was drawn to him. He wasn't handsome in the conventional sense; he was boyishly good-looking and he had a charming smile. Tedo had a unique ability; he had great persuasive skills and he could convince almost anybody if he puts his mind to it. This is an impressive talent, an ability that could have propelled Tedo to become a good public speaker, an excellent psychologist, or even a renowned motivational speaker but he did not realize who he was. He could have used his persuasiveness to benefit himself and the people around him; but do you know what Tedo does? Tedo woos any and every girl he sees for the sole aim of adding them to his sexual conquest diary.

Unbeknownst to Tedo, he really did have a gift, but he was using it in ways contrary to what the Creator planned, he was abusing his gift/ability. And when your friends are also the blind following the blind, instead of pitying you when you are on your way, about to fall into the ditch, they will be right behind you shouting your praise.

How alarming is it when somebody who was born to be a great leader does not realize it? Tedo was supposed to be a man many people should be looking up to for counsel. His genius ability that should have transformed him to an individual in an influential governmental or administrative position was being wasted on sexual conquests and gratification. He belittled his gift and he used it for something of vain reward and useless purpose. He was abusing his life and he was thinking he was a 'Casanova'.

On a particular occasion, Tedo was dared by 3 of his friends to try to catch this hard-to-get lady that just moved in down their estate. "We know you have no chance whatsoever of having sex with her, Tedo; you have always claimed that there is no lady you cannot capture with your charming spell but this will be your downfall" All of Tedo's friend knew he was good with the ladies, but Chika — the lady in question — was different from Tedo's usual conquests; for one, she was from a wealthy home and she was on a completely different financial level from Tedo and his friends. She didn't hesitate to let all the guys that have approached her know that she was familiar with all their tactics, right before she sends them on their way. Tedo's friends had no doubt he was going to fail in his bid.

> *He that walks with the wise shall be wise but the companion of fools shall be destroyed.*
> **PROVERBS 13 V 20**

Do you realize that Tedo's friends were part of the elusive complications in his life that he had no idea about? There is a great wisdom in the book of proverbs that says "he that walks with the wise shall be wise but the companion of fools shall be destroyed". It is either your friends help you in recognizing the genius within you, and motivate you to use it for the right purpose, or they actually encourage you to engage in activities that will render your genius ability as a pitiable object of abuse or as a showcase of redundant wastefulness of amazing potentials. Show me your friends, and I can tell who you are — the people you surround yourself with can have a tremendous influence on your ability to discover the genius within you, and they can greatly and positively affect your inner drive to develop your latent potentials to the level that it makes a bright shining star out of you.

Days after Tedo's friends dared him, they visited Tedo at his place. As he opened the door for them, he smiled widely and said, "Perfect timing guys. I was hoping you guys would come around today." "Why is that?" they chorused. He ignored their question and ushered them in. Lo and behold, reclining on his chair wearing only Tedo's shirt with shorts was no other than Chika, the girl nobody else could get close to. His friends couldn't believe it, "how did you do it?" they asked him later on. He laughed and said with a sense of triumph, "I have a gift my friends, my tongue is coated with honey and no girl can resist me!"

What a distasteful and a disgusting waste of a God-given ability! What an abhorrent abuse of an amazing potential! Do you know that this is the way many youths are wasting their lives on frivolous activities today; on events that do not add any value to the lives of people around them? Have you also been mindlessly and ignorantly emptying the gems of your precious life into gratifying but useless and unproductive endeavors? It is high time you accept responsibility to begin to live a transformed lifestyle, a life that will use his or her extra-ordinary gifts and talents for purposes that will glorify your Creator; a life that will make certain that none of his or her genius capabilities resident within will be unexploited; a life that will avoid the regretful end of amazing genius capabilities expended in futile efforts of a mind filled with vanity.

You may be a ladies' man today, but have you thought about other ways you could be using your ability more effectively; more profitably? Will being a 'ladies' man' give you a sense of profound fulfilment in life? You must take a step back and re-evaluate your life; your ability was given to you for more important things, and you must cease from wasting or abusing it. You can no longer hide under ignorance; now that you know better, you must do better. You owe it to your Creator to use the abilities He gave you for the right purposes; you owe it to yourself not to waste your abilities and your life, and you owe it to your country and your continent; this country needs more people who have discovered and are committedly developing their genius ability to go forward and it begins with you! In the next few chapters, I will be showing you practical steps to take in order to discover and develop your genius capabilities.

GOLDEN NUGGETS
FROM CHAPTER 4

- Sometimes, the worst of all men is the one with the best ever seen potential.

- The worst of all incarcerations is knowing that you have genius abilities but you cannot find any way to express it according to the design of your Creator.

- If we have discovered our unusual and supernormal abilities, only through WORK can we be able to utilize them for maximum benefit to mankind in spite of obvious limiting challenges that seem to stop other people.

- Without putting in necessary work, you will not be able to overcome the overwhelming temptations of using your great potentials in the most negative ways. Hard work and persistence is what distinguishes the shining star from the hopeless criminal.

- Work is one of the most marvelous inventions of the Creator. Without it, one would be condemned to a useless and a frustrating life.

- The talents that were put in you by your Creator are like seeds; it takes work to develop them to the point of fruitfulness and flourishing to your world; no other short-cut can get you there.

- Selfishness is a deadly bug that will never allow you maximize your potentials. You cannot keep thinking of yourself alone and expect the light of your genius ability to shine to your generation.

- If you are engaged in a negative work, it will eventually catch up with you and hamper your destiny; you cannot get anywhere far with a negative lifestyle.

- Your genius was designed by God to be used NOT for despicable, immoral and corrupt activities; your genius was designed to bless the lives of people around you and make this world a better place.

- True greatness will keep eluding you in life if you do not make up your mind to use your genius abilities exactly for the things they were designed to be used for.

- It is quite possible you are abusing your genius ability without consciously being aware of it; a deliberate and introspective appraisal of the use of your talents will help you make an informed decision.

- An ability or talent that you are despising or abusing is the same one someone else has believed in, and has committed to achieve great accomplishments with.

- There is a great latent genius capability in everyone, it only needs an unusual level of commitment and dedication to WORK in order to reveal the genius we are created with.

- It is either your friends help you in recognizing the genius within you, and motivate you to use it for the right purpose, or they actually encourage you to engage in activities that will render your genius ability as a pitiable object of abuse or as a showcase of redundant wastefulness of amazing potentials.

CHAPTER 5

THE THINKING POWER OF A GENIUS

From when he was a young boy, Trey was always a deep thinker, and on many occasions, his parents wondered how a child of his age could ponder things with such profoundness. Trey was constantly contemplating the inner workings of everything around him and wondered about things everyone else took for granted; on top of all these, he had a vivid imagination. Whenever Trey and his family were to go out together, he would be the last person to get ready, and on one of such occasions, his mother called out to him, "Trey what are you doing down there?" he replied her, saying, "I'm thinking, mother. Don't you ever think?"

After reading the story above, what was your first reaction? Did you think "wow, that's a rude kid," or did you stop and contemplate the question he posed to his mother? Forget about Trey's tone for a moment and consider this; if you were asked the same question, "don't you ever think?" what would your reply be? How many hours per day do you really spend in silent reflection? Do you ever just stop and think about how the world works? How often do you think deeply about the things around you? There is a correlation between constant thinking, exercising the brain, and genius ability, and if you ever hope to discover your genius ability, then you must spend a great deal of time in deep thought. No matter how much ability you have, if you don't spend some time thinking, you'll never be able to discover or harness it.

'Trey' in the story above is none other than Bill Gates as recounted in his book *"Showing up for Life"*; Trey was his nickname as a child. As we all know, Trey grew up to be a world-renowned tech billionaire and one of the most influential men in the world. There is no doubt that Bill Gates is a tech genius, and considering the fact that he is the richest man in the world, there must be some business genius up there as well. Given how much time he spends thinking — as seen from the short story above — his genius ability isn't a thing of surprise. If Gates spent so much time thinking as a child, how much more do you consider his thinking capacity would have grown since then? Don't you also find it interesting that the more he advanced in age, the more his thinking capacity grew, and the more he was able to realize his incredible potential? Ergo, the more he was able to accomplish great things with his genius ability!

> *Thinking is the hardest work there is, which is probably the reason why so few engage in it.*
> HENRY FORD

A lot of people have not discovered the genius in them because they don't spend enough time utilizing their brain, they don't exercise their minds; and as a result, whatever abilities they have remain locked. Are you one of such people? Nobody is born a genius; geniuses are made through personal endeavor, and thinking is a pivotal part of this

THE THINKING POWER OF A GENIUS

effort. Rather than spend valuable time in the deep recess of their minds, rather than make use of their thinking faculties, most people will rather spend their time doing mindless and repetitive labor. Do not be deceived, without spending time harnessing your thinking power, you can never discover your genius ability. Henry Ford confirms this as stated in the quote above that people rather go do physical activities because they are running away from the most difficult of all kinds of work, which is thinking.

> *Five percent of the people think; ten percent of the people think they think; and the other eighty-five percent would rather die than think.*
> THOMAS A. EDISON

Thomas Edison was quite observant, and he gave us a wonderful insight into the reason why it seems as if there are just few geniuses in this world. He knew that the problem was with the thinking habit of humans. The Creator gave all of us equal brains but what separates the top 5 percent of the world from the remaining 95 percent is not the ability to think (we all have it); it is the willingness and accepting the responsibility of thinking. It is quite appalling to know that 85 percent of the world would rather die than think. Do you want to remove yourself from the league of ordinary and common man? If you want to elevate yourself to a height of notable significance, you do not have any other choice but to start consciously and with disciplined efforts start using your brain to think. If devotion to physical work is the way to become highly eminent and relevant on this earth, brick layers and heavy construction laborers would have been the most impactful people on the earth. People who are mostly prominent and outstanding because of their work are ones who discover and develop more of their genius capabilities by using their thinking power.

Please take note that there are three kinds of work: *spiritual work, mental work and physical work*. Out of these three kinds of work, mental work is the one that mostly makes you relevant on this earth. It will interest you to know that God created man as a spirit but he decided to additionally give soul (mind) and the physical organ (brain) to man. He gave man brain as the instrument to subdue this earth and have dominion in the physical world. Spiritual work is used mainly to be in touch with our Creator, and as good as it is, without mental work, we cannot fully come to the understanding of what the Creator is getting across to us.

Many religious people who have focused on just spiritual work have made themselves largely irrelevant and useless on this earth. They fail to see that mental work is what gives value to any kind of spiritual work done by humans. No matter what is revealed to you from the spirit realm, it takes mental capacity to make it a reality in the tangible physical realm. No matter how much you are devoted to spiritual work, if you do not spend time to use your brain and think diligently, you will not be able to be the head in any sphere or aspect of the society. The greatest and the most influential people on this earth are people who use their brains regardless of whether they are religious or spiritual.

Friend, there is no better way to start discovering the great potentials that you already have within you than deciding to start doing the hard work of thinking. The surest way to elevate yourself to be among the top 5 percent people in this world is to become dedicated to mental work in addition to any other types of work you may be doing.

WORRYING VERSUS THINKING

Worry is a misuse of the imagination.
DAN ZADRA

Gabriel harbored dreams of being an Engineer in the future, but he was starting to give that dream a rethink. The reason is; he was terrible at mathematics and despite how much he tried to grow an interest in it, it was all in vain, and his space at the bottom of the math class was all but assured. Because of his struggle with it, whenever it was time for math, Gabriel found it hard to concentrate; he worried that he would never be able to understand, and before long, he gave up trying to understand it, "My brain was not made for solving math," he told his friends. What Gabriel did not know was that he was misusing his imaginative capabilities as Dan Zadra said in the quote above. Our minds and imagination are a great tool that the Creator gave to us; but we will not understand how much we are capable of doing if we are misusing it.

When it was announced on the assembly ground that the Secondary School Leaving Exam was just some months away, a new fear gripped Gabriel's heart, "How am I going to pass mathematics," he wondered silently, "I can hardly grasp the most basic concepts, how will I pass a standardized exam?" He stopped eating and was wearing himself thin with worry. In desperation, he began to cram formulas but despite that, he couldn't apply any of them to solving problems. One day, he got so frustrated that he began to cry. His teacher walked in at that moment and saw him crying. "What's the problem, Gabriel? Why are you crying? Is everything okay? Amidst tears, he explained his dilemma to her and she sighed as she sat down beside him. "Mathematics is a very easy subject, but it is also the subject that gives students the most problem, do you know why?" Gabriel shook his head as she went on, "many people find mathematics difficult because it requires thinking, and unlike some subjects that you can cram your way through, to excel at mathematics, you need to use your thinking faculties. People do not like to think, rather, they do what you have been doing, they cram."

Let our advanced worrying become advanced thinking and planning.
WINSTON CHURCHILL

"I want you to try this as from today; before you start trying to solve math questions, take deep breaths and ignore everything around you, focus inward and give all your attention to what is front of you. When you study the example, don't just read it and skim through it, digest it; make sure you understand the example thoroughly; it is only by doing so that you can apply the knowledge gained from the example to solving other questions." In a nut shell, the lesson from Gabriel's teacher can be applied to all other aspects of human life and it is best described by Winston Churchill's quote above — no matter how far you have become advanced in worrying, you can turn the situation around and convert it into an advanced thinking and advanced planning. Advanced worriers focus on their challenges and problems (without being able to make progress), while advanced thinkers concentrate and keep on pondering on ways to provide solutions to their problems; and they move a step forward at a time by utilizing their mental energy positively.

When Gabriel applied the method his teacher shared with him, he started to find that math wasn't so hard. On occasions, he'd find a question so tough that he'd begin to worry; however, all he had to do is refocus his thoughts to solving the question and away from worrying about the question. As soon as he does that, the question became solvable. Gabriel couldn't believe math could be so easy for him, he'd spent all his life thinking he wasn't made to know mathematics; he had been so wrong.

The illustration using Gabriel's story is just one of many around us that can show you the difference between thinking and worrying. Do you — like Gabriel — spend so much time worrying about something that you don't have the time to think constructively about it? How much of your life have you spent worrying about one thing or the other, as opposed to the time you spent thinking about how to make those things better? You may believe that merely contemplating on an issue is the same as thinking about it, but you're wrong. Think back at those times you've spent ruminating; were you thinking of solutions? Or were you worrying about the problem? Any time you spend worrying is a time that could have been used on profitable thoughts; if Bill Gates had spent all his time worrying about succeeding in his endeavors, how much time will he have left for productive thinking or to accomplish his purpose? The habit of worry is what get many people running around and busy doing what they are not supposed to be doing. For example, when you worry too much about your survival and the well-being of your children, you will not even take time to think creatively and productively proffer solutions to the problems confronting you. All you want to do is to secure any kind of job without any regard to how well you can use the genius ability within you to help not just yourself and your family, but several more people that your ability can serve. John Maxwell puts it well when he said:

> *The greatest enemy of good thinking is busyness.*
> JOHN C. MAXWELL

To realize your genius potential, you must be a deep thinker, and the biggest enemy of valuable thinking is useless worrying. You'll never find a genius saying things like, "Oh no, that question is too hard, how do they expect us to solve it." Instead, you'll hear things like, "it may seem very hard right now, but once I spend some time thinking about it, I'm sure I'll figure it out." Can you see the difference in the thought process of a genius and that of someone who is a worrier? Which are you? Are you a worrier? Or a thinker?

> *Instead of worrying about what you cannot control, shift your energy to what you can create.*
> ROY T. BENNETT

Everyone has incredible abilities within but worrying is an ugly impurity the covers the treasure of the great genius we were originally destined to manifest. One of the greatest fallacies of life that have hampered the ability of many to discover their genius and work at developing it is the falsehood of worrying habit that feigns itself to be real thinking. This was the case of Gabriel — he never knew he could be so good at math; he allowed worrying to rob him of his glorious destiny for years. People expend so much energy worrying, and when you ask them, they tell you they are thinking. No one gets anywhere in displaying exceptional capabilities if all he is busy doing is worrying and not actually solving problems. People that get excited at solving problems have exceptional thinking capability. Roy Bennett said it well in his quote above: the same energy it takes to worry is the one it takes to create positive solutions. Everyone who worries is using the energy of his thoughts negatively instead of using such energy for creative purposes.

> *Whoever is careless with the truth in small matters cannot be trusted with important matters.*
> ALBERT EINSTEIN

Let me give you a little more context — If a machine gets faulty just before production deadline, are you the type to break down with worry, or will you rather spend time to creatively think of ways to either fix it or replace it? If you have lots of projects to complete with little time, will you spend all your time worrying about how little time you have, or will you try to figure out a way to do more in less time? These may seem like trivial questions right now, but I assure you, these seemingly minor things are what separate the acclaimed geniuses from the common man. Albert

Einstein, one of the greatest minds of all times says in the quote above that you will never be trusted with important things if you are careless with the truth in small matters; paying attention to details and applying your mind to creative thinking in small matters can distinguish you beyond your imagination among your peers. If you ever hope to discover or harness your genius ability, you must learn to do the hard work of thinking like geniuses do.

ARE YOU A LAZY THINKER?

> *We all have ability, the difference is how we use it.*
> STEVIE WONDER

Let me tell you about Jessica who was the whiz at her stockbroking firm. All her bosses held her in high regard, and her colleagues considered her as a genius and looked up to her. The reason for this is; Jessica was so good with numbers that she does her calculations manually and still finishes before her colleagues that use computer software. While her co-workers struggle to input the data and run the software, Jessica just pored over the sheets with her pencil, and after some minutes, she was done. After months of speculation about how she does it, her colleagues concluded that she was "special," "She's one of those gifted people who can do unnatural things," they all agreed. As a result of her speed with her calculations, she usually has more time, and was able to get more things done than all her co-workers; she even had more free time. They all thought she could do what she did because she is a genius and nobody ever asked her how she did it, they all believed, "She's not like us." Imagine! They did not know that they all had this same ability, but as Stevie Wonder said, the real difference between people is how they get to use their different abilities.

One day, curiosity made one of Jessica's colleagues, Maureen, ask, "Jess, how do you do it? How can you calculate faster than a computer program? I've been wondering about it for a while now and I just can't help but ask you. Jessica smiled wryly and answered, "When I first started working here, I used the software for all my calculations too but one day, I wondered if I could do the job more efficiently than the software. So, I did the calculation using my brain and I realized that using the software wasn't very much faster than doing it manually; don't get me wrong, the software calculates faster, but when you factor in the time used to input the data, you'll realize that it saves you time doing it using your brain. When I started doing the calculation manually, I wasn't as fast as I am today, but with time and practice, I got faster. I also found that I enjoy utilizing my brain, and unlike the software, when you use your brain continually, you add value to yourself; continuous calculation using my brain is what made me a numbers genius today."

Maureen then realized that she — and most of her colleagues — were lazy thinkers. They didn't want to use their brains in doing multiple calculations because there was an easier way of doing the same calculation, and they never stopped to consider if using their brain was faster. She decided to try out what Jessica told her and she found that it was true. Maureen also found that there was a feeling of accomplishment when she used her brain, and before long, her boss and her co-workers became flabbergasted that she suddenly became a numbers genius too.

> *Don't be trapped by dogma... living with the results of other people's thinking.*
> **STEVE JOBS**

This story of Jessica is simple but yet, profound. In this story is the answer to the curiosity of many people as to the difference between geniuses and ordinary people. Every great genius you see in our world today are people who take their time to think. They do not just blindly follow what others are doing without doing the necessary mental work that will prove to them that they are moving in the right direction.

If you have always done some things without even asking yourself if there is a better, quicker, more effective, and more efficient way of doing it, then you are depriving yourself and others of your genius ability. If you accept blindly when people tell you the best way to do things, instead of pondering on it yourself, you may never be able to manifest the amazing potential that the Creator already put within you. Steve Jobs gave us an insight into what made him one of the greatest technological innovative minds ever; he said he was not trapped by dogma, he wasn't living by the results of other people's thinking; he took responsibility to think by himself and decided to do things differently. Because of his hard work of thinking as a personality and not following the band wagon, he created an exceptionally relevant group of companies with some of the most sought-after brands in the whole world.

Dear reader, please refuse to be one of those people that don't want to use their brains and would rather rely on alternative means or the results of other people's thinking efforts; the fact of life is that the more you use your brain, the sharper it becomes. Jessica in the illustration above discovered that technology might not necessarily make your job faster and that the thinking power of a human brain can be underutilized by believing that computer software will always be faster. A good lesson to pick from her story is that the fact that things have always been done in a certain way is the more reason why we should do the hard work of thinking about how it can be improved or done in a much smarter and creative manner.

Maureen — like most of her other colleagues — was underutilizing her brain as a result of overreliance on technology, and until she talked to Jessica, she didn't realize that the reverse was the case. An average person believes technology is faster than the human mind, and often, as true as that belief may seem, this is what stops people from discovering and maximizing their genius ability. We are now in a world where phones have become smarter than human beings. If you get too soaked in the practice of overdependence on smart technologies and you are not exercising your brain, you may be leaving a great treasure resident inside of you untapped and continuously regard yourself as incapable despite the amazing potential that the Creator has put inside of you.

If Jessica hadn't invested a few minutes into thinking and quickly experimenting, she wouldn't have discovered that she had it within her to do a faster job than the computer software did. If she had followed the average or lazy thinking of her co-workers, she wouldn't have discovered her incredible ability with numbers. Your thinking may be the only thing holding you back today from becoming the best version of yourself; geniuses are diligent enough to think differently when compared to the average person, and this 'difference' is part of the reason they're regarded as geniuses. If you want to be acknowledged as a genius, never be too reluctant or lazy to use your brain.

I was in Israel one day, and I, together with some of the Jewish people were taking a ride to have a good view of the landscaping around. We were driving across Israel while they were showing me the difference between the houses of Jews compared to the houses of Arabs and the Palestinians. It was amazing to see that the Jewish quarters had so many trees and green fields; these houses were accommodating so many beautiful trees; they looked very similar to my house in Ukraine. When you visit my house, you see a wonderful landscaping and the beautiful trees. The Jews are more civilized and they know that it's not just about the beautification of one's house and surroundings. Being a friend of one's environment is also important. This is because we all need to live in places that can contribute to our better health; we all need oxygen-rich atmosphere. Science has proven to us that people who live around trees live longer, and their health is better because they are inhaling purer oxygen.

I found out that the Palestinians don't plant trees; they prefer to do landscaping with flowers but not with trees. What they do not realize is that — it is what you put outside the house that has a bigger role to play in determining the length of your life than what you put inside the house. God put these together from creation and he even made it available to Adam and Eve in the Garden of Eden. Now, what I want to bring to your attention is that the people that spend their time to think about what is happening around them; people who take time to think and find out what ways they can live the best of life will not just assume or start copying what everybody else is doing. The brain of an Israelite is not different from that of a Palestinian. God did not make the brain of an American more developed than that of an African. We all have equal brains. The quality and the magnitude of time we spend in thinking is what differentiates us from person to person.

People who engage in real thinking will know that trees are not meant to be cut down haphazardly. And I have observed a similar trend of negligence to the environment about my country, Nigeria. Years ago, a friend of mine wanted me to buy a house in an estate in Nigeria. And the house was going to cost me a million US dollars. Many of my friends from England had bought houses in this particular estate, and they were encouraging me to buy as well. So, they sent me photographs and videos of the house. I was shocked to see what the house looked like; I exclaimed: "Is this a desert?" This place was a forest before so they went ahead and cleared the forest; they removed all the trees and just built their houses. They only planted flowers but they did not take their time to think and realize that flowers don't give oxygen; flowers are majorly built for beauty and for our eyes to behold. In the estates people build these days, people just put concrete and cement everywhere. In Ukraine, we have trees close to 400 years old. The longer the trees live, the better for you and the community. Peo-

THE CREATIVE AND INNOVATIVE POWER OF A GENIUS

ple come around and trim them, and cut the branches to keep them safe. But in some places, they take caterpillars and tractors and just cut them off. This is simply because people don't take their time to think. We should take time to think and ask ourselves questions about what we read even in the Bible. Why did Adam and Eve have plants and trees all around them in the Garden of Eden? It was because God, the designer understood the role of plants and trees in human life.

Productive thinking by leaders in Africa, for example, will lead to the maximization of all the resources our great countries have been blessed with; and our nations would be better off economically, socially and all other ways. If the artisans and small business-owners are able to think productively and harness their exceptional abilities, their products and services will be of such a high value that they would be in demand both at home and abroad; making our continent an industrial hotbed. It may seem hard to believe, but all we need to do to propel our countries to the zenith of national development is for everybody to start engaging in productive thinking. If I do it and you do it too, believe me; we're well on our way.

According to a report put out by the National Bureau of statistics in 2016, over 26.06 million Nigerians are either unemployed or underemployed. While it is certain that many of these people do not have the necessary qualifications to tie down a good job, among them are hundreds of thousands of people that are graduates of one higher institution or the other. Can you imagine how much the nation could benefit from millions of people using their brains productively? Don't you find it ironic that as much as people complain about unemployment, there are people out there starting profitable businesses and using their brains to make a good living? The reason for this is simple; as evidenced in Jessica and Maureen's story, most people will rather not use their brains because they are lazy thinkers.

Apart from what they were taught in the classroom, many graduates are bereft of ideas and irresponsible to do productive thinking. In fact, most graduates dished out by universities in many countries today can hardly defend their certificates. Sometimes, you meet higher institution graduates and you wonder if they even attended high school. It is indeed saddening that so many people will rather starve in hunger or steal than use their brains. Your mind is your secret to a life of prominence and relevance on this earth. The more you neglect its use, the greater the sorrows and woes of life you deliberately subscribe to.

The world we live in today is one in which most people remain average because they haven't unlocked the door of their ingenuity, and this is taking its toll on different nations. When you start following the practical wisdom exposed in this book, you will break away from the chain of mediocrity, you will unleash the power of productive thinking, and your genius ability will shine through.

As a student, do you believe that you can be the best among your peers? Do you know you can be the foremost accountant at your firm; the best engineer in your field or the best doctor in the country or the most innovative inventor the world has ever seen? If you do, then you must know that the only step between you and achieving that your dream is simply doing the hard work of harnessing the power of your brain. Once you unlock the door of productive thinking, the incredible genius ability the Creator put in you will be made manifest.

IF YOU ARE NOT THINKING, THEN YOU ARE ASSUMING

*The essence of the independent mind lies...
in how it thinks.*
CHRISTOPHER HITCHENS

The great genius ability within you lies in the fact you will be able to use your mind to think independently of other people's opinions. You will not just base your life on mere assumptions that the direction most people are moving is the best direction to follow. We know geniuses because they discover more excellent ways of doing things than the ordinary man knows; this kind of genius capabilities only shine through to the outside world for responsibility-conscious people and the diligently thinking minds.

I like to share with you the story of Ahmed and Toyosi who were childhood friends and despite the disparity in their backgrounds, they did everything together. Ahmed applied to study Law and Toyosi, Economics at the University of Ibadan. Because Ahmed was denied admission in the university they both applied to, they became finally separated; while Toyosi went to the University of Ibadan to study Economics, Ahmed went off to a private University where it was easier to secure admission.

The Thinking Power of a Genius

On graduation, both boys were faced with the popular issue of unemployment that plagued the country and they spent some time at home while they waited for word from few of the many interviews they'd done. On a particular afternoon, Toyosi asked Ahmed what he felt about starting a business venture in their community. "What would we do? Ahmed asked with little interest. Toyosi ignored his friend's nonchalance and said, "I don't know yet, but I'm sure if we give it some thought, we can figure out something our community lacks. That is how all great businesses start, someone sees a need and he/she moves to provide for that need." Ahmed shrugged and said, "I can't be stressing my brain or wasting my time thinking about that; my Dad may be retired, but he still has enough influence to help me get a good job. You can waste your time thinking about one business idea or the other, but I can't." Toyosi chuckled and changed the topic, he was hoping he could change Ahmed's mind if he would eventually come up with a good idea, and he had no doubt he would figure out something interesting enough to get his friend's attention.

Two weeks later, Toyosi was back in Ahmed's house with unusual excitement. He had a wonderful idea that he was certain would turn his friend's head, an idea he thought would compel Ahmed to invest some of his money, time and efforts. However, he was shocked when Ahmed shot the idea down, "That can't work," he said, "Nobody will buy building materials from us. They all have suppliers in the city" Toyosi couldn't believe his ears. He said "I have given this some thought, I've done some research and I'm certain that if we can get enough money to purchase directly from the manufacturers, we can offer cement and other materials at prices that will be beneficial to us and the builders close to us. Think about it, we will save them the stress of going to the city whenever they need something, and we also save them transportation costs." Ahmed shook his head stubbornly and said, "If the idea is so great, why hasn't anybody tried it? What if the manufacturers refuse to sell to us? Even if they did, how will we transport from their plant to our little town?" It was at this point that Toyosi gave up trying to convince his friend; he couldn't believe Ahmed could be so mule-headed that he didn't see what was right in front of him. Ahmed didn't even give the idea some thought, he just assumed right off the bat that it wouldn't work. However, Toyosi decided to seek help elsewhere.

> The third-rate mind is only happy when it is thinking with the majority. The second-rate mind is only happy when it is thinking with the minority. The first-rate mind is only happy when it is thinking.
>
> A.A. MILNE

According to A.A. Milne in the quote above, Ahmed had a third-rate mind. He was only comfortable with thinking like the majority is thinking. But Toyosi's mind was a first-rate mind, at least relative to his locality. He dared to do what nobody else around him was doing because he took responsibility to think when others were priding themselves on their assumptions. There is no way for you to fly high in life if majority of your beliefs and world views are assumptions. Imagine that your pilot is flying a plane several miles up above in the sky based on assumptions and not on proven facts and principles, how calm and easy do you think your flight will be? You sure know it will be a hell of a flight, and that is if you ever get to make it to your destination. Life is not meant to be lived by assumptions; life is lived based on discoveries and principles well understood by the quiet thinking attitude of a diligent mind.

In 6 years, Toyosi had happily expanded his building material venture to the surrounding areas and he was the biggest supplier around. He was a wealthy and accomplished young man. He'd built a house for his folks, and all his siblings were well taken care of. His business was doing even better than he'd envisaged and was in the process of opening a megastore in the city. One day, Ahmed came to Toyosi's house and he complained bitterly about how hard life was, "I should have listened to you, Toyosi, and I should have at least given your idea some thought. We could both be rich and comfortable right now, but look at me; I regret my decision till this day."

Friend, I must tell you this — the plight of those who do not take their time to think is usually *regrets* at the end of the day. They regret seeing other people doing what they had assumed cannot be done. They regret coming across people they thought had inferior abilities but are now doing greater things than they could ever imagine. What makes average people 'average' is how they think, they prefer to assume than to utilize their brains doing the hard work of thinking.

A person who knows the importance of deliberate mental work and applies himself to it can never be average, and when people see the result of his expansive personal research and intensive observation, in conjunction with his productive thinking, they regard such a person as a genius. An average man, on the other hand, will prefer to make unintelligent assumptions, he will see excuses in every opportunity and rather than think up solutions; such a person would say things like, "If nobody else is doing it, why should I?" This is the type of thinking that relegated Ahmed to a life of regret while his friend became a business magnate. People who don't know their story will see Toyosi and think, "that man is a business genius," they wouldn't know that the only difference between Toyosi and Ahmed is that, one of them applied the power of his thinking faculties, and converted an opportunity into a business venture, while the other preferred to assume things won't work rather than think productively.

> *The world as we have created it is a process of our thinking. It cannot be changed without changing our thinking.*
> ALBERT EINSTEIN

If you are one of those people who find it hard to apply your God-given intellect, life may inevitably be hard for you. You should know today that the only remedy to a hard life is the hard work of thinking. How many opportunities have you missed by dismissing things without giving it some thought? If you are underutilizing your brainpower so much, you don't have any other choice but to live an average life. I implore you to learn a lesson from Toyosi and Ahmed's story. While geniuses think of how to make things work, average and ordinary men will rather stay idle and live with the assumption that smarter people would have already utilized the idea if it was really viable. Albert

Einstein puts it well in the quote above, when he said you create your own world with your own thinking; whether you are average or you are exceptional in life is as a result of your thinking. When you change your thinking attitude, you change your life.

We started with the story of Bill Gates; he is a man that lives above the dangers of costly assumptions. In the 1980s when Bill Gates wanted to start Microsoft, people laughed him to scorn and told him nobody would buy a computer software. Even when he outlined his beliefs — as a result of careful consideration and painstaking research — that it would be profitable to sell software separately from hardware, everybody thought he was insane. Today, Bill Gates is the wealthiest man in the world and Microsoft is the foremost software company in the world. What if Bill Gates had accepted the assumptions of the people that tried to dissuade him? He might have ended up living the average life. My friend, the more assumptions you follow in life, the greater the probability of you remaining in mediocrity. Decide today to start doing the hard work of carefully analyzing your facts and stop the lazy attitude of religiously accepting and living by assumptions.

How can I make this work? What can I do to improve this idea? Is there a way I can get this done faster? These are the thought processes of geniuses. They weigh things in their minds and think productively till they arrive at a desirable answer. Ignorant people will rather assume that since everybody did it in a particular way, then that must be the best way to do it. But when these unlearned people see others do things differently and get it amazingly right, they term them geniuses and say, "they were created specially," or "the Creator endowed them with a special brain." They'll make even more gruesome assumptions and will fail to realize that the only thing that differentiates them from the geniuses is how they think. As humans, we are all given equal brains by the Creator; everyone just uses theirs differently. Will you continue to lead an ignorant life? Or will you revamp your thinking process and tap from the genius ability that is in you? The choice is definitely yours to make.

You have learned from the story of Toyosi and Ahmed but it is good to see how great scientists utilized the power of thinking to find out the reason behind natural occurrences that ordinary men were trying to understand, but never went beyond the level of assumptions. Isaac Newton is worth mentioning here, because as a young student at Cambridge University, he wondered constantly about a concept he later called gravity. His breakthrough didn't come in the laboratory; neither did it come to him when he was studying in the library. Newton cracked the mystery of the earth's gravitational force in his mother's garden — when an apple fell on his head and got him thinking. Newton is today regarded as one of the most influential scientists and it is mainly as a result of his work on the theory of the earth's gravity. Don't you find it ironic that he was spurred to make one of the biggest scientific discoveries of his life in a garden? This is a testament to how constantly and diligently he thought about it; how he dedicated virtually every living moment of his life to solving the problem because he refused to be living by assumptions; rather he used the ever-available mental resource of the human brain to provide solution to the problem that has been begging for answer for many years. You have also been given this same gift and resource of a wonderful brain, but no one can use it on your behalf; you just have to decide to use it by yourself and make a difference in this life.

Have you heard about Albert Einstein's "thought experiments"? Einstein would relate scientific problems to real-life situations and things he could see around him. Using his "thought experiments" Einstein was able to lay the groundwork for his special theory of relativity, and solve many of the other scientific issues that proved elusive to him and many others for years. Albert Einstein knew that sometimes, thinking can prove to be much more productive than doing physical experiments. He also realized that thinking was not supposed to be a one-time or a periodic thing, he knew he had to think constantly if he hoped to achieve anything profound in life, and in the end, he achieved an unprecedented level of results with his life. He would use the "thought experiments" to think up solutions, and he would go back to his lab and work out the the science. Just as stated in the quote below, science has more to do with thinking than it has to do with the body of knowledge and philosophies people are already celebrating. Nearly all the most important scientific discoveries of all times were more largely a product of mental work than physical work.

> *Science is a way of thinking much more than it is a body of knowledge.*
> CARL SAGAN

If you have regarded thinking as something you only do occasionally, then you're on your way to a mediocre life. People who are regarded as geniuses today are those who realize the importance of thinking, as opposed to worrying or assuming foolishly. These people don't think only when they are in a good mood, they create their own pleasant moods by constantly thinking, regularly doing mental analysis and as a result, they are respected as the best among their contemporaries and even remain relevant for multiple generations.

Now you have realized that the majority of the work you need to do to be truly exceptional in life is mental work; it is high time you changed your attitude towards better and more focused mental exercises. You can't sit around and expect insightful ideas to fall into your laps without the hard work of thinking; you become more productively relevant in life as a result of diligent and strategic thinking.

I believe that if more Africans are thinking productively, then there is no limit to what we can achieve as a continent. I hope you now believe with me that we can use the power of thinking to raise our nations up to the lime light that we have long desired; and we can be removed from the position of mediocrity that we have been relegated to; if we all harness our brainpower and continue to do productive mental work, our lives and our great nations will not suffer any more but begin to benefit massively. In the next chapter, I will be showing you yet another powerful habit you need to inculcate to unlock the creative genius within you and develop it to outstanding heights of significance.

GOLDEN NUGGETS FROM CHAPTER 5

- A lot of people have not discovered the genius in them because they don't spend enough time utilizing their brain, they don't exercise their minds; and as a result, whatever abilities they have remain locked.

- Nobody is born a genius; geniuses are made through personal endeavor, and thinking is a pivotal part of this effort.

- The Creator gave all of us equal brains but what separates the top 5 percent of the world from the remaining 95 percent is not the ability to think (we all have it); it is the willingness and accepting the responsibility of thinking.

- If you want to elevate yourself to a height of notable significance, you do not have any other choice but to start consciously and with disciplined efforts start using your brain to think.

- People who are mostly prominent and outstanding because of their work are ones who discover and develop more of their genius capabilities by using their thinking power.

- Spiritual work is used mainly to be in touch with our Creator, and as good as it is, without mental work, we cannot fully come to the understanding of what the Creator is getting across to us.

- No matter how much you are devoted to spiritual work, if you do not spend time to use your brain and think diligently, you will not be able to be the head in any sphere or aspect of the society.

- To realize your genius potential, you must be a deep thinker, and the biggest enemy of valuable thinking is useless worrying. Everyone who worries is using the energy of his thoughts negatively instead of using such energy for creative purposes.

- Everyone has incredible abilities within but worrying is an ugly impurity the covers the treasure of the great genius we were originally destined to manifest.

- One of the greatest fallacies of life that has hampered the ability of many to discover their genius and work at developing it is the falsehood of worrying habit that feigns itself to be real thinking.

- No one gets anywhere in displaying exceptional capabilities if all he is busy doing is worrying and not actually solving problems. People that get excited at solving problems have exceptional thinking capability.

- If you have always done some things without even asking yourself if there is a better, quicker, more effective, and more efficient way of doing it, then you are depriving yourself of your genius ability.

- If you accept blindly when people tell you the best way to do things, instead of pondering on it yourself, you may never be able to manifest the amazing potential that the Creator already put within you.

- The fact that things have always been done in a certain way is the more reason why we should do the hard of work of thinking on how it can be improved or done in a much smarter and creative manner.

- If you get too soaked in the practice of overdependence on smart technologies and you are not exercising your brain, you may be leaving a great treasure resident inside of you untapped and continuously regard yourself as incapable despite the amazing potential that the Creator has put inside of you.

- The plight of those who do not take their time to think is usually *regrets* at the end of the day. They regret seeing other people doing what they had assumed cannot be done. They regret coming across people they thought had inferior abilities but are now doing greater things than they could ever imagine.

- A person who knows the importance of deliberate mental work and applies himself to it can never be average, and when people see the result of his expansive personal research and intensive observation, in conjunction with his productive thinking, they regard such a person as a genius.

CHAPTER 6

THE STUDYING HABIT OF A GENIUS

There are more men ennobled by studying than by nature.
MARCUS TULLIUS CICERO

When the result sheet was given to Ben, he didn't bother to look, and while the other kids in his class go from one person to another asking what position they were in the class, nobody came to his seat. He did not mind, he didn't need the hassle, and everyone knew what position he'd be; it's the same position he'd always been for the past 3 years. The only year he took a break from being in the last position in the class, it was only to climb one place as the second to the last boy, and the next year, he regained his position as the 'class dullard'. Even though one or two kids still make fun of him, it was a fruitless endeavor; Ben had resigned to the fact that he was the dullest kid in the class, and making fun of him just wasn't fun for the other kids anymore. What Ben did not know, as at then, was the truth in Marcus Tullius Cicero's quote above — that it is not nature that really ennobles men; men actually become dignified by their habit of studying.

On his way home, his spirit plummeted; even though most of the people around him no longer cared about his results and academic performance, his mother was one person who was still interested. He braced himself for what was to come after she sees his most recent performance; outrage, anger, accusation and afterwards, a plea to him to do better. On getting home and on showing her the result, he was met with an entirely different response; instead of the usual emotional outburst, his mother just smiled sadly and continued what she was doing. Over breakfast the next morning, the hammer dropped; apparently, his mother's reaction the previous evening isn't a signal that she'd come to accept that her son was a dullard. She announced that as from that day, Ben and his brother were to follow a strict schedule; they could no longer play or watch TV, instead, they would do their assignments, study their notes and when they were done with that, they would get a book from the library — whichever book they wanted — and read. Only after doing all that could they play.

Ben felt like he was being punished and he rebelled a little bit, but his mum didn't relent, and as time went on, the new schedule became law. After a while, Ben started to notice some changes; the more he read, the less he felt like a 'dullard'. Could it be that the reason he'd always been a dullard was because he didn't study? He wondered privately. He started to feel a certain power the more he read and his mind-set started to change; before long, he started to realize that he really wasn't dull and that all the classwork that seemed so hard were that way because he didn't study. In the past, he had no plans for the future, however, the more he read, the more he realized that there was no limit to what

The Studying Habit of a Genius

he could achieve; the more he studied, the more he knew that the only difference between him and those he regarded as smart — those he thought were geniuses — was how much they studied.

Then one day in class, his teacher asked a question and nobody in the class knew it, even the 'geniuses' that topped the class; nobody except Ben. When he raised his hand, I'm sure some of his mates may have snickered, after all, if the smartest kids didn't know it, how could Ben? To the surprise of the teacher and his classmates, Ben got the answer correctly. Apparently, Ben had read it in one of the books his mom 'forced' him to borrow from the library every week. From then, he found himself looking forward to the next book; it was a thing of surprise for Ben that the only thing he needed to be a genius was to study. It was at that moment that his life turned around, and he began to lead his class.

'Ben' is none other than the highly respected neurosurgeon, Dr. Ben Carson. Yes, Ben Carson was once the dullest kid in his class. However, when he discovered the studying habits of geniuses, his life turned around for better. He went from being the dullest to being a medical genius; no other thing but studying got him there. Dr. Carson was once quoted as saying,

> *I started reading about people of great accomplishment...and it dawned on me suddenly that the person who has the most to do with what happens in your life is you.*
>
> Dr. Ben Carson

Ben Carson made the greatest discovery of his life when he began reading about people with great accomplishments. He realized that every man's destiny is in his own hands, and no longer in the hands of the Creator. It is whatever you sow into your life that you reap as harvest. Dr. Carson began sowing the hard work of studying and reading into his own life and he began reaping the reward of a great genius capability. On graduation from high school, Ben Carson earned a full scholarship to Yale — one of the best schools in the United States; a notable achievement for someone who was once the 'dullest' person in his class.

Has everybody written you off and concluded that you would always be the worst student or professional? Have you also resigned to the fact that you're a 'dullard'? Well, the story of Ben Carson should have convinced you better about how wrong you may be. The renowned neuro-surgeon once said,

> *Every person is endowed with God-given abilities, and we must cultivate every ounce of talent we have in order to maintain our pinnacle position in the world.*
> DR. BEN CARSON

If there is any person you ever need to listen to about the miracle-transforming power contained in the habit of studying, it should be Dr. Ben Carson. This man literally discovered that there was a great genius within him, even as he had failed all his life, and he was able to use this exceptional ability he found in himself to elevate himself to the pinnacle of his career. The Creator puts genius ability

The Studying Habit of a Genius

in every one of us; he gave us the ability to be the top in whatever field we are in, all we need to cultivate that genius ability is to be given to the habit of studying. Those people you regard as geniuses are those who spend their free time studying while you watch TV or you are mindlessly surfing the internet, these are the people who know that genius comes with study and as a result; took the time to develop their brain.

Ben was termed a 'dullard' and it was so bad that he even believed it; but that 'dullard' rose to the top of his class, that 'dullard' got a full scholarship to one of the best universities in the world, that same 'dullard' became one of the best neurosurgeons the world has ever seen, and the 'dullard' has been able to save the lives of lots of people; he achieved all these by doing the hard work of studying; the world termed him a dullard but by developing a voracious studying habit, he proved them wrong. What are you waiting for? Having read Carson's story, it will be irresponsible to keep on thinking you don't have the genius ability within you. All you need to do now is to cultivate and develop that habit. What you need to do is to study hard; study till you discover your genius. It does not matter what age you are right now, if you will begin to study at least one book per week in your area of interest, you will no doubt turn yourself into a sudden miracle genius. You need to harness that genius ability; your family needs you to do it, your country and the whole world is waiting for you to manifest.

You are a genius, the only reason you haven't discovered it is because you haven't studied enough; when you begin to push yourself beyond your limits by doing the hard work of studying and thinking, you will regularly be coming across several treasures that the Creator has embedded within you from birth. Until you shake off the belief that you were created differently from those with genius ability, until you come to terms with the fact that you have the genius ability inside of you already, you will not be motivated and dedicated enough to bring out the great and wonderful potential within you. Being a genius is the original design of the Creator for everyone; nobody was born a 'dullard'. To be recognized and acknowledged as a genius, you must adopt the studying habits of brightest minds of this world; but to study as a genius who you are, you must first know that known geniuses are normal persons who decided to study harder and think harder than ordinary people.

> *I was a normal person who studied hard.*
> RICHARD FEYNMAN

Feynman was a great genius who has been credited with pioneering the field of quantum computing, and introducing the concept of nanotechnology. He developed a widely used pictorial representation scheme for the mathematical expressions governing the behavior of subatomic particles, which later became known as Feynman diagrams. During his lifetime, Feynman became one of the best-known scientists in the world. In a 1999 poll of 130 leading physicists worldwide by the British journal Physics World, he was ranked as one of the ten greatest physicists of all time. This man knew he was just a normal person like everybody else, as in his quote above, but the most important quality that distinguished him as one of the best scientists of all times is the habit of studying very hard.

If we encounter a man of rare intellect, we should ask him what books he reads.
RALPH WALDO EMERSON

You have remained at the level you are for many years not because you are inferior; neither is it because you are disadvantaged; and believe me, it is not because of the witches and wizards of your father's house; you may have only remained at the same level because you have not taken time to develop yourself and add substantial value to your life by immersing yourself in the diligent habit of studying. The truth cannot be further stressed than contained in the quote of Ralph Waldo Emerson above; every man of rare intellect (like Richard Feynman) that you will encounter anywhere has definitely given himself to the habit of reading to become so. The more relevant books you study, the greater the wisdom and the knowledge at your disposal. All the people that are regarded as geniuses are people that spend a lot of their time studying, people that read far and wide, people that seek to gain insight from everything and everyone who has got some needed wisdom around them. Please realize that studying is one of the principal keys that unlocks the door of the genius ability within you.

SHOW ME A GREAT GENIUS WHO DOES NOT STUDY

Yes! Show me a great genus who does not study, and I will tell you he does not exist. I will be giving you several additional examples of amazing geniuses in this section and all of them became extra-ordinary, super normal, and exceedingly exceptional because they chose to devote themselves to the habit of studying. Who you are and who you will become is absolutely a matter of your choice.

Let me start with Elon Musk, who is one of the brightest minds of this generation. He is an Engineer, an Inventor, a Designer and much more; a genius no doubt. He has pioneered many new technologies and he is in the process of launching even more. Even though he's just 45, during his life, Elon Musk has mastered the technology behind on-line payments (from when he co-founded PayPal), rocket flight (his company SpaceX was the first privately-funded company to build a rocket), electronic car manufacturing (Musk owns Tesla, the biggest electric car manufacturer in the world); all these from a man that studied Physics and Business in the university. When asked on how he could master so many unrelated fields in so little time, Musk said, "*I read books.*" He was also quoted as saying,

> *I think many people can learn a lot more than they think they can. They sell themselves short without even trying.*
> ELON MUSK

If you see anyone that never opens up books to read, the person is selling himself short and is not even trying to learn. Musk always emphatically says it that there is nothing special about him. He knows that he would not be what he has become today if he has not given himself to the habit of reading. According to entrepreneur.com, Elon Musk was reading for 10 straight hours when he was in grade school; he read everything he came in contact with, including the entire Encyclopedia Britannica. Musk was said to enjoy studying the way other people enjoy watching television.

The Studying Habit of a Genius

Let me ask you a question — if given an option right now, will you rather study or watch television? Well, Elon Musk would have chosen to study; that's why he's highly regarded as a genius, and you should know that studying and continual learning is the main difference between him and every other ordinary person who has not been able to achieve much significance with their lives.

> *Natural abilities are like natural plants,*
> *that need pruning by study...*
> FRANCIS BACON

Elon Musk must have known that he was smart; he might even be aware that he was a genius, but he kept reading. Why? The answer is simple; being a genius is more about hard work, especially in the form of studying, self-education and personal development than anything else. Musk self-developed himself a lot to get to where he was, but even when the world knew and respected him as a genius, he still kept at it; this is because the only way to keep developing your genius ability is by studying. From Bill Gates to Albert Einstein, to Isaac Newton and Leonardo da Vinci; all famous people with pronounced genius abilities are also known to be chronic readers. These men recognize the power of self-education and they cultivated a habit of reading as much as possible. If self-development is the key that gets you into the hall of fame of geniuses, it is also what keeps you in that league and makes you produce even more with your life. Francis Bacon summarizes it in simple but profound words as in his quote above — your natural abilities need to be pruned like natural plants in order to remain relevant on this earth, and one of the best ways to do it is through studying.

> *Study hard what interests you most...*
> RICHARD FEYNMAN

Richard Feynman hits the nail on the head again — you don't need to be struggling to study; just focus on your area of interest. Geniuses do not view self-education as an option; neither do they see it as a punishment because they know that therein is the secret to their greatness; they study hard because they love to; because they enjoy it. To develop your genius ability, you must enjoy studying, and you must make it a second nature. Albert Einstein once said to his son,

> *That is the way to learn the most...*
> *when you're doing something with such*
> *enjoyment that you didn't notice that the*
> *time passes.*
> ALBERT EINSTEIN

Until you get to a point that you have developed a strong liking for self-education and you are doing it with so much enjoyment that you do not even notice the passage of time, then you can be assured that you will be able to produce results comparable to that of Elon Musk, who is among the top one percent of the people in the world in terms of impactful, entrepreneurial, innovative and technological achievements.

Friend, I want to tell you that if you discover your genius ability early in life, that is the more reason to even devote

THE STUDYING HABIT OF A GENIUS

yourself to the habit of studying relevant books and assimilating important materials in your area of interest the more. Even though Musk has gotten to a point in his life and his career when he could afford to stop pushing harder like many other people would do; he is now at a point where nobody doubts his genius; but he has not stopped working hard. Instead, he is always seeking more knowledge in order to break new grounds; he is highly devoted to the habit of acquiring knowledge and he continues to develop his brain.

The studying habit is the hallmark of geniuses. And I must reiterate it again that if you want to continually grow your genius capability, if you want to achieve success with your mind, if you want to use your intellect to impact the world; you must view self-education as an enjoyable act, you must see studying as food, and personal development must be part and parcel of your life; that is the way geniuses do it, and there is no other way to rise to the pinnacle of your career.

I am going to mention Isaac Newton again, and even more, as we proceed in this book. He was a man that touched our world in an unusual manner, and we need to learn a lot from him. He was described as "studious" by his biographer, John Conduitt. Conduitt went on to say that Newton always had a book in front of him or a pen in his hand except when he was involved in "business or civilities of life." No wonder he was known to be such a remarkable genius; he utilized the open secret every other genius makes use of, it is none other but the studying habit.

"Just about every kind of book interested him — encyclopaedias, science fiction, you name it. I was thrilled

that my son was such an avid reader, but he read so much that Bill's mother and I had to institute a rule: no books at the dinner table." These were the words of Bill Gates' father in a recent interview with Forbes. Is it any surprise that Gates turned out to be such a genius? From when he was a child, he loved to read, and he read far and wide; imagine how quickly he was developing his brain. He read everything he could lay his hands on, he read every time of the day, and as a result of his incessant studying, Gates discovered his genius ability early in life. When he noticed he was a genius, that didn't make him stop, in fact, his studying intensified.

When in College, he read with a greater voraciousness. His Harvard roommate once described Gates' studying habit, he said, *"his habit was to do 36 hours at a stretch, collapse for 10 hours, then go out, get a pizza, and go back to it."* It is no wonder that he is one of the smartest minds of this generation. Can you read for even 5 hours at a stretch? Gates studied for a day and a half at once. No wonder he's such an unusual genius.

Till date, Bill Gates still a glutton for books like he was as a kid. His blog "GatesNotes" features over 150 books on varying topics; from novels to historical books and lots more. Gates is rumored to read about 50 books per year, and even when he goes on vacation, he goes with his books. Browsing through his online book blog, you're going to find books that touch on many aspects of life and living — motivational books, historical texts, political biographies and a host of others; books that keep Bill Gates informed on all that goes on around; knowledge that can't be garnered except through studying. Is it surprising then that he has great success with whatever he undertakes? Can you imagine how much insight he has gained by reading so widely? Friend, it does not matter how much time you are spending to wish and desire greatness in life; your only chance of extra-ordinary accomplishment is your dedication to the hard work of studying, reading, thinking, and self-development, through which you can gain all the insight you need to make a head way in life.

> *Never regard study as a duty but as an enviable opportunity to learn, to know... and to the profit of the community to which your later works belong.*
> ALBERT EINSTEIN

Also, it is very crucial to consider the reading habit of Albert Einstein, who is one of the smartest men in history. His name has almost become synonymous with the word 'genius'; young students often coin nicknames out of the name 'Einstein' as a way of showing a great admiration for the man. Because of how greatly history revered him, many people find it hard to believe that they can be as smart as Einstein; they believe his genius ability was endowed from heaven; they attribute his ability to some mysterious gift. The truth, though, is in his quote above — Albert Einstein became so smart by being committed to learning, and his exceptional abilities were developed from a certain attitude to self-education; he did not see studying as a duty, instead he saw it as an enviable opportunity to learn. Wow! Imagine the thoughts of a great man, *"studying is an enviable opportunity"* and I must tell you studying is also what will make you become enviable in life just like Einstein.

But note that you also can recreate some of Einstein's habits; you can become smarter, and you can increase your intellectual abilities. You only have to do what Einstein did; you only have to spend time in incessant studies like Einstein, then you can come out with amazing discoveries. You may not be a theoretical physicist, but whatever you aim to succeed at in life, you must implement a strict studying regimen, you must self-develop yourself beyond what an ordinary person does; study with all your heart, without distraction, and in a manner that confirms that the secret to your great accomplishment in life is in addiction to learning.

When Oprah Winfrey started her show "Oprah's book club" in 1996, she did it to encourage the average American on the importance of reading. She knew how important studying was to personal growth, and she knew that if more Americans read more books, it would go a long way in advancing the country; she was right. The show received good reception and throughout the 5 years that it ran for, over 55 million copies of the books featured on the show were sold. Oprah looked around her and she saw that people didn't realize the importance of reading to both personal and societal development, and she decided to do something about it.

It was said of her effort, *"Oprah is a serious American intellect who...took reading ...and highlight its social elements and uses in such a way to motivate millions of erstwhile non-readers to pick up books."* Africa and Asian third world countries need people like Oprah Winfrey; people who know the importance of reading and personal development and how it impacts national development. Im-

The Studying Habit of a Genius

agine how beneficial it will be for our great nation if more people are self-educated, imagine how much more geniuses our dear country will produce if everyone has recognized the immense benefit of studying. It is not coincidental that the developed countries in the world are those that encourage reading the most. There is a popular saying that goes thus — *"if you want to hide something from a black man, put it in a book".* I will encourage every black person to prove this saying as wrong as possible. When your life begins to produce amazing and unexpected results, everyone will come and ask you what books you are reading.

Warren Buffett once said the secret to his success was to read "500 pages every day." He added, *"That's how knowledge works. It builds up, like compound interest. All of you can do it, but I guarantee not many of you will do it."* Buffett himself estimates that he spends 80% of his working day studying and reading. There is no doubt that Buffett is a man with a lot on his plate; he has a company to run and lots of other businesses to attend. Despite that, he still spends more than half of his day reading one book or the other, from several pages of business reports, to economic reports, as well as financial news and magazines; Warren Buffett recognizes the importance of staying informed through self-education and he takes time out of his busy schedule to study. No wonder he is called the *"wizard of Omaha,"* no wonder he is a business genius, one of the greatest investors in the world.

At 86-years of age, and as busy as Warren Buffett is, he still endeavors to develop his brain by reading and studying. What then is your excuse? Do you have as much on your plate as Buffett does? How many hours a day do you spend reading? Buffett spends approximately 80% of his day studying, and for a man that has a lot of responsibilities, that is a sizable chunk of his day. I'm certain you most likely are not as busy as Warren Buffett, but you still find reasons not to study. If you don't adopt the studying habit that is working for geniuses, how do you hope to be acknowledged and recognized as one by your world?

In January 2015, Mark Zuckerberg made a decision to read and complete a new book every fortnight. He even started a "Year of Books," a book club on Facebook because he wanted to discuss the books he read and how they impacted him to the Facebook community.

All these are not isolated examples. Steve Siebold interviewed over a thousand millionaires and found that they all had a habit in common; they all loved to read. These are men whose genius ability is not in doubt; men in the higher echelon of personal and financial accomplishment. Isaac Newton, one of the pioneers of science and mathematics, Bill gates, one of the wealthiest and most influential men of our time, Warren Buffet, the most successful investor in the world, and Mark Zuckerberg, the founder of the biggest social networking site in the world; they are not all in the same field, but they are the best at what they do. These men have two things in common; they have incredible genius ability, and they owe it to incessant studying. What are you waiting for?

SELF-EDUCATION LEADS TO AMAZING DISCOVERIES

Thanks to the discovery of airplane, we can all travel around the world. The advent of airplanes has made it very easy for cross-continental migration and we are all able to fly all over the world. The idea to build airplanes first came to the earth and the minds of men by observing and studying nature; men were able to decipher a mystery from nature through the hard work of studying and self-development. Men began to imagine that if birds could fly, why is it that we cannot fly? Then, they started studying it through mathematics and through science. They started researching and they went through different ways just to discover how, why, and what is the secret behind the birds flying? They did an in-depth analysis, looking into what makes them fly and putting in hard work to gain a thorough understanding of the dynamics behind the flight of birds. They knew that if one could understand the principles responsible for the ability of birds to fly, it can be replicated. And surely, eventually, it was and has been massively replicated for enormous benefit all over the world.

Let me give you another example of treasure that was discovered through hard work — how did we come about cars that we all drive around today? The car was invented through careful observation and studying animals; men started to look deeply into why animals run faster than men. The strength and the speed of horses were put into major consideration. Hence, the term, horsepower was coined. Man decided to study the speed of horses and he came about cars. There is no way you would be committed to studying and not discover the treasures of life, the treasures of nature, and the treasures of the earth. People have used the principle of hard work to give birth to cars and planes. Others began observing the whale and shark, studying and trying to understand which principles were responsible for abilities of motion under water. And boom! Man came up with the invention of submarines. All of us can become inventors over time, from one generation to another, if we will understand and develop this habit of purposeful studying and self-education. When we continually do this, the present generation will just be building on the knowledge transferred from past generations. This can only happen if we commit to the art of self-studying to understand beyond the levels of past generations.

> *Study to show yourself approved, a work man that needs not be ashamed, rightly dividing the word of truth.*
> II TIMOTHY 2 V 15

As the Bible quotation above puts it, if you want your life to be full of glory instead of shame, you simply need to be dedicated to the habit of self-education, rightly diving (analytical thinking). This is how to live a life that would be acknowledged by top professionals and experts in the society. And they will begin to seek you for your wisdom. For example, I did not study physics and neither was I taught chemistry in school. But I am dedicated to self-education, and because of this, even a professor of Chemistry at an American University told me that he never understood chemistry until he met me. This is what self-education can do to you. I know that treasures are around us and within us if we decide to study and work hard. Humans are the most treasured people on earth and every effort of humanity is to discover man, to fix man, and to make life much more comfortable and interesting for man on the earth. What are you using your own life to do? Why don't you invest your life in hard work?

I like to encourage you to challenge yourself with making an amazing discovery in your area of choice, and watch your genius potentials begin to manifest into physical realities. I discovered nobody has ever written one thousand books in their life time and I said I am going to be the first one and I am already on my way to doing it. I am going to write my first one thousand books in ten years and I am going to exceed it. It's easy to do because I have given myself to a lot of self-development and therefore, I have so much to offer to my world.

Right now, my goal is to change a nation, not just one nation, I want to change nations; I want to subdue nations for God; I want to raise up men who are deliverers, history makers, and shakers of this world. It is true that this is my own area of specialty, as it is my field of calling. But discovering your calling and your assignment on earth is not just enough. Your committed hard work is very essential. Therefore, I have worked in diligence in the labor room of studying and self-education, adding so much value to myself to be confident enough to transform a whole nation for God. And I have already proved the validity of this truth in the nation of Ukraine; so it is an easy thing for me to make economic and political transformation happen in Nigeria. When people hear the confidence with which I speak, they cannot but be overwhelmingly amazed; it becomes a great puzzle to figure out how I will transform a whole nation.

What we all need to realize is that we can all develop our genius abilities if we will convert our time into tremendous added value to ourselves in form of self-education.

We're all gifted with exceptional ability and all we need to unlock it is to study and self-educate. When unlocked, however, you mustn't rest on your oars, because studying will help you discover your genius ability, but once you stop studying, your development stalls, and before long, you'll find yourself languishing in averageness. I believe you have learnt one of the greatest secrets of amazing geniuses from this chapter. The next thing I want to show you is that even the least privileged of all persons can do amazing things with his life if he is committed to the discovery and the development of his genius capability, and I will be using the story of my life to prove this to you. See you in the next chapter!

GOLDEN NUGGETS
FROM CHAPTER 6

- The Creator puts genius ability in every one of us; He gave us the ability to be the top in whatever field we are in, all we need to cultivate that genius ability is to be given to the habit of studying.

- You are a genius, the only reason you haven't discovered it is because you haven't studied enough.

- When you begin to push yourself beyond your limits by doing the hard work of studying and thinking, you will regularly be coming across several treasures that the Creator has embedded within you from birth.

- You have remained at the level you are for many years not because you are inferior; neither is it because you are disadvantaged. You may have only remained at the same level because you have not taken time to develop yourself and add substantial value to your life by immersing yourself in the diligent habit of studying.

- If studying is the key that gets you into the hall of fame of geniuses, studying is also what keeps you in that league and makes you produce even more with your life.

- Geniuses do not view studying as an option; neither do they see it as a punishment because they know that therein is the secret to their greatness; they study because they love to; and because they enjoy it.

- If you want to achieve success with your mind, if you want to use your intellect to impact the world; you must view studying as an enjoyable act, you must see studying as food, and studying must be part and parcel of your life.

CHAPTER 7

HOW I DISCOVERED MY OWN GENIUS

If you have made it to this point, I hope you have started sensing my intense passion for seeing everyone discover the genius that is within, and that the only way to discover and develop it is through hard work. Therefore, in this chapter, I want to paint a vivid and a graphic picture, using the story of my own life. I believe my life's story is such that can prove to anyone that everyone has genius capabilities; you may only be seen as a dullard or a nonentity if you have not realized the great treasures within you waiting to manifest. On the other hand, it may be that you know the amazing capability within you but you have not decided to be diligent enough to make it shine forth undeniably.

For many years and consistently, I was always at the bottom of my class. If other students or teachers were asked to point out the person with the emptiest head in the class or school, I would be one of the most nominated persons. The worst part of it was that I believed what everybody else felt about me; of course, my very poor grades did not let me think otherwise.

Let me give you an example — When I started primary school at about 4 years of age, my teachers were teaching me how to read. They tried their best but I just couldn't get it. When I look back, I get surprised at how they kept moving me from class to class, even without being able to read. Imagine someone not able to read; it simply means little or no education was taking place. My first breakthrough at reading came when I was ten years old — that was how backward I was in life.

Everyone was telling me I was so dull; I had no doubt too that I was really dull. It was very much later in life that I realized that the people telling me that I was dull were extremely wrong. I realized that I was too ignorant and naïve to be thinking that I was dull. This is why today, I cannot afford to just keep watching people thinking they are dull or inferior; I have now found out that no one was created to be dull. Everyone is a genius; only that it remains dormant until it is discovered and developed.

For instance, everyone was trying to teach me to read, and I couldn't get it. But none of my teachers considered to see if trying a different approach to learning would have worked out well for me. When I later discovered myself, I found out that my best method of learning is through critical thinking. The way I reason is much different from the ways others reason. My teachers just wanted me to learn in the same manner that others were learning; but the more they tried, the duller I became.

Are you beginning to see that some of the things you thought you were so terrible at learning may be because you were not provided with a method of learning that works best for you? If this were so, there is a great chance that you would have been one of the best among your peers or in your profession today. It is when you begin to discover yourself that you start realizing the best ways you learn. And the more you discover yourself, the better you can bring out the best out of you.

MY GREATEST DISCOVERY

One day, my sister came to visit me in the village where I was schooling, and through her, I made the greatest discovery of my life. The discovery I made through my sister on that day laid the foundation for a gloriously fulfilled destiny that has become an inspiration to many today. After this encounter with my sister, I rose from the bottom of my class to the top within few months. *"If you don't pass your school leaving certificate examination, you will remain in this village forever and you will just become a farmer; you will become one of the lost people in this village and you will never get out of here..."*, said my sister. Her words ignited a passion inside me and strongly motivated me to be ready to give it all it takes to rise above mediocrity.

I was so ready to do anything she would tell me to do, just to get out of that village. This was the village where I was born and I had been all my years. All my life up till that point in time, I never had a single pair of shoes. I was passing through so much suffering such that the energy level with which I was going to pursue any opportunity that will get me out of that village was unprecedented. I was so eager to discover any formula that would give me a chance to pass the necessary exam which was my only exit strategy from the village.

My sister led me through the Scriptures and showed me from Deuteronomy 28 that the will of God for me was to be

The Creative and Innovative Power of a Genius

the head and not the tail. I couldn't believe my ears. *"Do you mean it is very much possible that I can also be the head?"* I asked my sister. Then she replied with a very positive affirmation that it was indeed possible, and that is what God wants for me. This was the point my life change forever; I never thought in my life that I could be the best — that was the strangest idea from my thoughts. She told me God can help me to become the best if I do the things I was supposed to do. Then, I made up my mind to start studying hard from that moment. I had to do the hard work of running away from my friends because I knew with their presence, I would not be able to convert my time into knowledge to actualize my desires.

I was in a village that did not have access to a constant supply of electricity. Therefore, I would use our local technology (called lantern) to serve as a source of light for me to study in the room in which I locked up myself. I would stay up in the night and study till 2 am, and sometimes till 3 am in the morning. After doing this for a year, I suddenly rose to become one of the best students in my class.

> *Success is the result of hard work...*
> COLIN POWELL

Can you see any similarity between my story and that of Ben Carson as relayed in Chapter 6? All my life before this point, I used to think I was born a failure in life. And I thought that others who were at the top of the class before I joined them were born geniuses; I thought they were just born smart. It was an amazing discovery for me; I did not know that all of us are born special in our own way. I did

How I Discovered My Own Genius

not realize that everyone on this earth is a genius and that you will not discover your ingenuity if you do not work really hard. I didn't know hard work brings guaranteed success with it.

Because I began pushing myself beyond my limits, when the results for final school leaving certificate examination came out, I had the second best result in the whole school. And surprisingly, I was the only one in my school who got a scholarship to study at a University abroad. Imagine how I would have missed an opportunity of a life time if I did not discover the treasure of work and applied myself to it. Friend, you are not worse than anyone; you can even do better than the people you are thinking are special human beings today. With all humility, I can say that I am doing better right now, than all other people that we started life together; and it is not because God destined only me to be great.

> *Winners embrace hard work. They love the discipline of it. Losers, on the other hand, see it as punishment. And that is the difference.*
> LOU HOLTZ

Like Lou said above, winners embrace hard work and that is why they are winners, losers see it as punishment, and that is why they keep losing. The difference between the people who are not perceived as geniuses and those who are highly exceptional is a major principle that the outliers work with: they choose to give the whole of themselves to achieve their desires and their purposes. In the process of doing this, they find more amazing things about themselves that they never knew existed before. Nothing pays like hard work!

You need to know that you cannot afford to be working hard without working smart. I did not have extremely low academic performance because I was lazy; I was working hard but I was neglecting the most important thing. I was working so hard in the farm; I was hawking and selling local food to take care of myself; I was hawking firewood. But I was adding no value to myself internally and mentally. I was absolutely ignorant enough to be ignoring the greatest form of work. Until you start working hard to add value to yourself, you may not be able to discover the hidden genius capability within you.

I can tell you that what is within you is beyond your imagination. There is so much treasure in you. Your potentials are not inferior to the capabilities of Albert Einstein; Isaac Newton did not have more treasures in him than you have in you. You are not worse than any of the great names you've ever heard about. You are very much as great as they were on the inside. They were only distinguished because they went ahead and pushed themselves beyond their limits and they were able to unveil the greatness resident within them. If you also don't diligently push yourself and work very hard as someone that really means business, you will never come to the actualization and realization that in this lifetime, nobody is better than you. If you do not adequately understand the virtue of diligence and hard work, it may be close to impossible for you to discover all the great and wonderful things you could have done with your life.

How I Discovered My Own Genius

Don't wait till you die before you discover your treasure, all the precious virtues hidden in you. If you could just take a decision to work extra hours and to work fourteen to eighteen hours minimum in a day, using your time to add value to yourself or converting your time to valuable products and services, then you are on your way to becoming an amazement to your world. When you start exercising the force of diligence in tilling your own land of promise and you keep at it, then you are ready to become a household name in your world. You do not have to be seeking for fame before your name becomes known all around the world just because you are able to solve a long-lasting problem for your generation.

There are so many problems in your country and you should be the deliverer. Your country is waiting for somebody to bring an end to unfavorable conditions and circumstances and all the solutions needed is buried within you. Until you accept this responsibility of being a problem solver and give unto it the right quantity and quality of work, you may not discover all your genius potentials and capabilities. Until you discover and start utilizing your genius, the solution you have inside you will remain useless to your country and to the world.

Your Success is in your Own Hands; it's Nowhere Else

Remember I said earlier that I got a scholarship to study abroad on the back of my impressive West African Examination Council (WAEC) result? Well, when I got to Russia, I was overwhelmed beyond belief and if you were in my shoes, you would have been too. As a young boy who grew up on a farm in a remote village in Nigeria, nothing prepared me for the life I was suddenly thrust into. There were over sixteen thousand students from 100 countries, and I wondered how I was going to cope, talk less of doing better than the other students. Also, growing up in Nigeria, I had the usual belief that the white man is smarter and better academically than the average African. On top of this, I was competing in a country where the language was alien to me. In short, I was very scared and there and then, I knew I was in over my head. To make matters worse, due to one reason or the other, I didn't resume with the other students and I was lagging from the get-go.

Before beginning my degree program, I was to undertake a one-year Russian language program. Can you imagine? I had a year to be proficient at a language and compete with students who had been speaking the language their whole lives. On seeing me, one of my lecturers, a white man, immediately killed the little morale I had left, he said, *"...you know you have missed so much, you will never be able to catch up... I've been teaching at the university for so long with many years of experience and I know my job. No student can make it with your kind of accent and being this late. You will never speak the Russian language. You say you are a Christian but God cannot help you. If you speak this language I will go to church and believe in God as well but even God cannot help you..."*

His words weighed heavily on my mind, but I reminded myself that my success is not dependent on the words of anybody; whether he is a professor or even a prophet. Rather than let his words discourage me, I took it as a challenge to become the best. You need to understand something; when I left Nigeria, I wasn't even very fluent in English, and my

How I discovered my own genius

English was strongly accented as it is for most people that grew up in villages. So, the challenge seemed insurmountable, but I remembered where I was coming from. I remembered that some years ago, I was the worst student in my class and on graduation, I was the best. I worked hard for the opportunity to study in Russia, and I vowed to work even harder to be a success there.

I recalled how back in Nigeria, everybody thought I was a dullard until I worked hard, discovered myself and proved them wrong. I used work to unearth my genius back then, and I was going to do the same, only this time, against even greater odds. Let me let you in on a secret, it doesn't matter where you're coming from, or what people say about you. As long as you are working hard to add value to yourself, the treasure buried in you will surely shine through.

> *I know you've heard it a thousand times before. But it's true — hard work pays off. If you want to be good, you have to practise, practise, practise...*
> RAY BRADBURY

I'm sure you've heard it so much now, that it seems like a cliché saying, but like Ray affirms in his quote above, hard work always pays off. There is nothing else that can unlock your genius potential like hard work. While in Nigeria, I read every day for three hours to discover myself. So, in Russia, I decided to work even harder, I increased my studying time from three to six hours. Every day for seven years, after leaving the lecture hall, I would go to the library and isolate myself there. I studied for six hours every day without fail; if we had classes from morning to evening, it didn't matter to me, I would still spend my six hours in the library. If I got hungry, I would eat in the library. I spent more time in the library than I did anywhere else, and I did this for seven years. I can tell you that it wasn't easy, there were days that I was so tired I nearly gave it all up, but I didn't. I studied hard and true for seven years and in the end, it was worth it. Another secret for you to always remember, hard work always delivers.

At the end of my seven years in the university, not only could I speak fluent Russian, I graduated as the best student in the whole university. Yes, I had the best result out of the sixteen thousand students from all over the world. I topped all the white students I previously thought were smarter, I topped all the students that had the advantage of knowing the language since their childhood. I, a boy from a remote village in Nigeria that could hardly speak fluent English when he got to Russia, graduated as the best student in the university. That is not all, twenty-five years after graduation, nobody has been able to break my record. I was able to achieve this feat because I worked hard.

Do you still believe that someone is better than you? Do you still think some people were naturally endowed to be geniuses? After reading my story, surely, you must realize how fallacious your belief is. I'm sure there were many students in the university who had been termed geniuses since their childhood days, students who had been the best in all the schools they've attended. In the end, they were bested by a boy that for most of his life had been termed a dullard. They could not compete with my work ethic, my insatiable hunger to discover and harness my genius potential blew them all away. That was when I recognized that my back-

How I discovered my own genius

ground is of little consequence to my success, what matters is the fact that every one of us has the same 24 hours every day. What you do with your 24 hours is what will decide how much you will accomplish on earth. While in the university, I used mine judiciously, and as a result, I discovered the priceless treasure within me. I overcame all difficulty and came out victorious.

Buried within you is a potential that is powerful enough to make you the next best thing the world has ever seen. You have the potential to be the next Bill Gates, the next Warren Buffet, but until you discover that potential and harness the ability, it will remain dormant. Nobody was created without an important reason; you were created for a specific purpose; I was created for a reason too. Through hard work, I discovered the treasure I had within, I discovered my ingenuity. Your treasure is waiting for you to do the same, I urge you to take the step that I did, use your work to find your treasure.

> *If people knew how hard I worked to achieve my mastery, it wouldn't seem so wonderful after all.*
> MICHELANGELO

Until you do so, you will continue to believe that people who are geniuses are more special than you are, but in truth, they are not. When you study for 18 hours straight for many years like Tesla did, you will realize that he really wasn't born a genius, when you dedicate as much to your work as Michelangelo did, you will come to find out that he wasn't created with a special brain. I said earlier that you have the potential to be the next Bill Gates, I said so because

I saw the manifestation of work, I saw how it could open facets of your mind you never knew existed. I worked hard because I wanted to uncover the treasures I had within, but believe me, when I saw what I was capable of, I was shocked. I couldn't believe I could do the things I was doing with ease; this is why I tell you with confidence, you have the potential to become the next great thing, all you need to do is unlock the treasures. The key, dear friend, is work.

DEVELOPING YOURSELF MAKES YOU STAND IN THE SHOES OF GREAT MEN

After I graduated, I was called into the ministry. Being a black man in a country that was predominantly white, I was worried that I would struggle to get people to listen to me. I knew that white people, as a rule, would rather not follow the teachings of a black man, and so, I wondered how I was going to succeed as a pastor under such conditions. But, at this time, I knew how to solve the problem, it was the same way I had solved all the problems I ever faced in my life. I looked within and went on a journey of self-discovery through hard work. In the end, I found the answer to my problem. White people, though wary of following a black man, could be depended upon to pick logic over sentiment. So I had a new challenge, I had to add value to myself, so much so that I could convince my congregation with examples backed by logic and hard facts.

I worked hard and developed myself to the extent that I could state my argument and use logical examples to convince anyone with lingering doubts. Also, if I was to have any chance of leading a church in Russia, I also had to polish my Russian. While in school, I was fluent in Russian, but to become a pastor, I had to do better, I had to lose any trace of my accent that lingered. I not only had to be able to speak eloquently in Russian, I also had to be able to speak without blemish. It took time and hard work, but I accomplished this too. When I had completed my journey of self-discovery and self-development, my church grew in leaps and bounds. When the congregation grew to thirty-three thousand members, I had successfully built the biggest church in Europe. If you have been following my story from the very start, you'll recognize how much of an accomplishment this is. From being the class dullard, I worked till I became one of the best students at my secondary school, the only student worthy of a scholarship abroad. On getting abroad, I worked hard and mastered a hitherto alien language. And not just that, I studied hard and graduated with the best result, a record that still remains, 25 years after my graduation.

> *The dictionary is the only place that success comes before hard work. Work is the key to success, and hard work can help you accomplish anything.*
> VINCE LOMBARDI

Did you see how much I was able to accomplish with hard work? Have you seen how much work transformed my life? Have you seen how I discovered treasure after treasure through hard work? All through my life, work has helped me achieve unprecedented feats. Therefore, I think I'm in a good position to tell you how much more you can uncover in your life if only you work hard. I can testify about the efficacy of work because I applied the same work to my life and I uncovered treasures beyond belief.

After a while, I had developed myself to the extent that I felt that I had nothing more to learn about being a preacher. I met with great preachers and I can humbly say that I outshone them all. I attended conferences with preachers I revered and I discovered that none of them were better than me as long as I worked hard. You see, there is nothing that tops hard work. Hard work is the master key that unlocks all treasures, all potential, all abilities. With hard work, I was unstoppable and there was nothing I couldn't accomplish.

Then I met Myles Munroe. When I listened to him speak, I was blown away. I couldn't believe it, here was a man I could listen to, a man I could learn a lot from. I started listening to his messages and I was developing myself even further. When we eventually met at a conference, I was billed to speak before he did, and when I was through with my ministration, Myles Munroe asked that I be allotted his slot. He said there was nothing else he could say, he just wanted to keep listening to my preaching; I could hardly believe my ears. This is what happens when you discover yourself when you use the key, which is work, to unlock the genius ability within; the men you look up to as great, as geniuses will come to regard you with respect. So, you see what I said about you having the potential to be the next great thing the world has ever seen? There I was, with the respect of great men like Myles Munroe and T.L. Osborn. My work got me there, but I wasn't satisfied. I thought to myself, if I can come from nothing and achieve all these, what more can't I accomplish with this work.

How I discovered my own genius

This, I believe, is the mind-set of great men. Men of great impact are never content with being the champion of one field, they want to test the limits; they want to conquer more spheres. My next challenge, therefore, was to be something bigger than a preacher. As a preacher, I was among the best, but financially, I wasn't all that. So I gave myself a target, I vowed to work hard and become a millionaire in 2 years. Nine months later, I reached the mark. The thing is, I was so used to working hard that I reached my goal in one-third the time I thought it would take me. So I asked myself, what else can I develop? I derived great pride from having reached my financial target with time to spare, so I decided to raise millionaires from my congregation. In three years, I had raised up about 200 millionaires from my congregation. Can you believe it? Not many years ago, I wasn't a millionaire myself, and not up to five years later, I was mentoring people to be financial victors.

> *All the so-called "secrets of success" will not work unless you do.*
> ANONYMOUS

There is no shortcut to discovering your genius ability, there's no big secret to it; it was the same tested and trusted hard work. Knowing the power hard work wielded was like having the master key to everything, and not long after, I was using my key to open another door. Before I mention what door it was, I want to make sure you understand that this hard work is available to you too. There's nothing to it, it is the same hard work that helped Nikola Tesla discover A.C. electricity. Tesla worked day and night in his lab to make it happen. He worked so hard, he could only afford

3-4 hours sleep every day. It is the same work that made Oprah Winfrey, a teenage runaway girl, one of the most influential women in the world today. Oprah started as a radio presenter and worked her way to the top of the ladder, till she owned her own TV network. Hard work is not an abstract concept, it simply means putting your work ahead of everything else, it means working so hard, your potential has no choice but to manifest itself into a full-blown ability.

The next door I opened was political relevance. I, the young man from Idomila village spoke in front of the most influential leaders in the world, and they gave their lives to Christ as a result of my charge. I spoke at the United Nations meeting with the secretary-general and again, at a meeting of presidents. I spoke at the Japanese and Israeli parliament; I spoke at the United States Senate, in front of hundreds of the most powerful people in the world. I had developed myself to the extent that the movers and shakers in all sectors wanted to hear me speak. A boy that was once the class dullard. You can also develop yourself like I did. In fact, I challenge you to do even better. Greatness is not a measure of anything else but the results birthed through hard work, and I can confidently tell you right now, you can surpass what I was able to accomplish. It all depends on how hard you're willing to work. From birth, we — you and I — have been imbued with all we need to make a great impact on our nation, and on the world. Whether or not you are able to harness that treasure for greatness depends on you and how hungry you are for greatness. You, however, cannot plead ignorance anymore. You know the truth, you have been given the key, it is now up to you to either open the door of your potential and harness your ability or continue to live in mediocrity. If I can go from being the laughingstock of my class to ministering in front — and touching the lives — of the most powerful men in the world, you have no excuse not to do better.

Now that you have learnt all it takes to be acknowledged by your world as a genius, I will be showing you through the next few chapters how you can take your genius further to the next level and begin to create, innovate, and invent. Surely, as you practice the principles shared in this book, you are on your way to having the best of time on earth.

GOLDEN NUGGETS
FROM CHAPTER 7

- Everyone is a genius; only that it remains dormant until it is discovered and developed.

- It is when you begin to discover yourself that you start realizing the best ways you learn. And the more you discover yourself, the better you can bring out the best out of you.

- Everyone on this earth is a genius and you will not discover your ingenuity if you do not work really hard.

- The difference between the people who are not perceived as geniuses and those who are highly exceptional is a major principle that the outliers work with: they choose to give the whole of themselves to achieve their desires and their purposes.

- Until you start working hard to add value to yourself, you may not be able to discover the hidden genius capability within you.

- You are very much as great as they were on the inside. They were only distinguished because they went ahead and pushed themselves beyond their limits and they were able to unveil the greatness resident within them.

- When you start exercising the force of diligence in tilling your own land of promise and you keep at it, then you are ready to become a household name in your world.

- If you do not adequately understand the virtue of diligence and hard work, it may be close to impossible for you to discover all the great and wonderful things you could have done with your life.

- Until you discover and start utilizing your genius, the solution you have inside you will remain useless to your country and to the world.

- It doesn't matter where you're coming from, or what people say about you. As long as you are working hard to add value to yourself, the treasure buried in you will surely shine through.

- Your background is of little consequence to your success; what matters is the fact that every one of us has the same 24 hours every day. What you do with your 24 hours on a daily basis is what will decide how much you will accomplish on earth.

- You have the potential to become the next great thing; all you need to do is unlock the treasures. The key is diligence.

- Hard work is the master key that unlocks all treasures, all potential, and all abilities. With hard work, you will be unstoppable and there will be nothing you cannot accomplish.

- Men of great impact are never content with being the champion of a single field; they want to test the limits, they want to conquer more spheres.

CHAPTER 8

ARE YOU A CREATOR, INVENTOR OR AN INNOVATOR?

Stanley sighed as he worked on the financial statements on his desk. He couldn't believe he was so fatigued, he peered at his watch and he was surprised to see that it was barely 10 a.m. "Argh!" he moaned, "How can I be so tired on a Monday morning?" He stood and left his office to get a cup of coffee, and on his way, he met Ibrahim, his colleague. "Are you okay Stanley? You don't look good." Stanley shrugged and answered with a gruff, "It's nothing; I just don't feel well." After some probing from Ibrahim, he caved and told him his concerns, "For some time now, I've been feeling like I'm underutilizing myself here" Stanley's hands spread to show that he was referring to the workplace in general, "like this isn't the path my life is supposed to take." Ibrahim's brows furrowed in confusion as he asked, "What do you mean? You are one of the best financial analysts at this bank; you've been Employee of the Year for 4 years running. You know what I think, I think you're mentally fatigued; it happens to all of us at one time or the other, get some days off work and relax, you'll be right as rain in a few days."

THE CREATIVE AND INNOVATIVE POWER OF A GENIUS

> *There is the happiness which comes from creative effort ...devising new invention, creating a vast industry.*
> HENRY MILLER

When Stanley got back to his office, he recalled his discussion with Ibrahim and he realized his colleague said something that struck close to home, he was indeed mentally fatigued, but not for the reason Ibrahim thought; he was mentally fatigued because he wasn't made for the kind of mindless labor he had been doing for the past 13 years. He had never felt fulfilled at his work and years of wading through and pretending that all was well beginning to take its toll on him. Just like the wisdom in the quote of Henry Miller above, Stanley had not been enjoying the happiness that comes from creative efforts, devising new inventions, and creating a gigantic industry. He had merely been living his life based on survival instinct like every kind of domestic and wild animals does. People that want to make a great impact in life do not live by survival instinct; they consciously work by principles and rules that will make them fulfill their purpose in life. One of such rules and principles is: *"In order to find true fulfilment in life, you must do the will of your Creator by making sure you contribute your own creations, inventions, and innovations to your world"*

Stanley's mind wandered to his days in the university. He was in the first year when he realized how good he was with solving mathematical problems; before the second week of the semester, he had already solved all the questions in his Advanced Mathematics textbook; even the questions that were earmarked as "extremely difficult" didn't pose too much difficulty to him. One day, his Math lecturer came

ARE YOU A CREATOR, INVENTOR OR AN INNOVATOR?

into the class and asked, "Who is Stanley?" when Stanley rose in response, the lecturer could hardly hide the shock on his face, "you're Stanley? The first-year student that solved the question I posted on the board?" Stanley nodded shyly. The lecturer asked him to come to the front of the class and he gave him a marker, "Please solve the question again, I still don't believe you solved it on your own." Stanley's hand was shaking as he collected the marker and as he wrote the complex equation on the board, but once he started solving, the shaking stopped and his confidence was unwavering; he was in his comfort zone.

When he finished, his lecturer asked, "Where did you learn that equation you used?" Stanley answered, "It's a combination of 8 formulas; the question was very complex and I knew it wouldn't have a specific formula, so I combined them all and came up with that," he pointed at the solution; it spanned the full length of the board. The lecturer was dumbfounded. His voice shook with admiration as he said, "The question that this boy — Stanley— just solved took 3 lecturers 2 months. I pasted it on the notice board to challenge the final-year and Masters students, and none of them have been able to solve it; in fact, nobody had submitted an attempt since I've put it up last week; up until today. The only thing I can tell you is; you have a gift. You are a mathematical genius, and as young as you are, there's no limit to where your ability can take you to. I have no doubt you will become one of the top scientists or innovators of your time."

Stanley wondered what that lecturer would say if he learnt where he ended up. He recalled when he got the job, his parents and siblings were over the moon, but he was

The creative and innovative power of a Genius

barely excited. He only took the job because circumstances forced his hand; his brothers had gotten admitted to universities abroad and his parents alone couldn't foot the bill. He thought he could live with working at the bank, but his time there had been hell. He was supposed to be innovating; his calling in life was to be inventive and creative. "I shouldn't be wasting my ability doing this mindless labor," he thought to himself, "I should be putting my mind to better use. I have been wasting my abilities."

Stanley's case is a very common occurrence all around the world. Young men and women with lots of promise and incredible genius abilities end up living for their salaries; all their talents and gifts that would have done a whole lot of good for this country becomes suppressed by mindless labor. They got caught in the rat-race for survival and their creative abilities are cast aside. Now, it is time for you to ponder on and answer the following questions:

- What have you been using your abilities for?
- Do you know that you are created to be a creator, an innovator, or an Inventor?
- Have been derailed from the path to your glorious destiny because you desperately want to survive?

> *My main purpose in life is to make enough money to create even more inventions.*
> THOMAS EDISON

If all you have been using your abilities to do is to secure good jobs because of salary or the sole purpose of your ability is for survival, it simply means you are just deliberately limiting yourself in life. I am not saying working at a job is a sin; but the life that the Creator has given is much more than mortgaging your life in jobs that will not allow you manifest all the creative, innovative, and inventive potentials that God has put within you. How do you think a Math Genius (as in the case of Stanley in the story we started with), who was created to solve the problems of his nation and the world at large by coming up with profound mathematical breakthroughs will be able to fulfil his destiny in the mindless labor of working in a bank just for salary and survival? The answer is in the quote of Thomas Edison above; Edison understood his purpose of making money as a greater opportunity to solve more problems in the world by coming up with even more inventions. He knew that there is no fulfilment of destiny if you are not doing what the Creator put you on this earth to do. If you do not make up your mind to convert all the creative genius capabilities that God has put within you into tangible value for the benefit of mankind, there is no way to fulfill your glorious destiny as either a Creator, inventor or an innovator.

> *...he that invents a machine augments the power of a man and the well-being of mankind.*
> HENRY WARD BEECHER

We were all created in the Creator's image, and as His Name proclaims, He is the **Creator**. It is important to note that since we were all created in His image, it is very safe to believe that we all have the ability in us to create, innovate and invent. Again, the important question is: have you discovered your creative ability? If you have discovered your genius capability, then you're already on the right path, all that is left now is to put in the hard work necessary to harness the creativity of your genius ability. The genius within you is the creative endowment that needs to grow into manifestation of the inventions within you. Henry Ward Beecher said in his quote above that when you do the work of invention, what you are simply doing is using your creative capability as a man created in the Creator's image, and by doing so, you are being of immense benefit to mankind. The truth is that we are all able to create and make new things; but if we do not decide to let this amazing potential within us grow into fruition through intensive hard work, there is no way we will be able to fulfil our destiny of the creation of new things.

For instance, how did we get to know that the Creator, God has the most profound extra-ordinary genius capability? We can see all His creations all around us; we can see the many wonderful things He made, and humans are still working day and night to figure out His wonderful handiwork. Yet, we have not reached even 1 percent success in trying to understand what a wonder he made of this world. God created the heavens and the earth in just six days; He worked very hard to produce unimaginable quantity and quality of creatures (both living and non-living) and He just had no option but to rest afterwards.

I want to remind you again that until you push yourself beyond your limits, you will not be able to produce the best creations of your life. It is through work that we are all able to recognize the greatness of God. Imagine the Creator of the heavens and the earth, emphasizing "work". Why did He not just speak those things He desired in His heart into existence? It is really incredible and heart-touching to know that even God as great as He is had to *work* to create everything (plants, animals, rock, sea, firmament, sun, stars etc.) that we see and we benefit from on the earth today.

Therefore, let no one deceive you — the only way you can amount to greatness in life is through work; if your Creator couldn't do it without work, how much more would you be incapacitated, fruitless and unproductive in life without work. As you have been told already, the reason why you were created in His image is for you to be a Creator just as He is. If you are not known as a creator, an innovator or an inventor on this earth, it simply means you are not fulfilling your destiny as a replica or an image of God. If you do not become dedicated to the hard work of creating just as your Creator was, there is no other way to express it apart from saying that you are wasting your life, you are wasting the precious gifts, talents, and abilities that God has put within you to do amazingly glorious things on this earth. I want to admonish you to refuse to be a waster; have a strong determination that you will give it everything it takes to fulfill your amazing and wonderful destiny as a creator.

I like to show you few examples of people who are harnessing the great creative potentials that the Creator has put within them. These people are proving through their hard work and diligence that they were indeed created in God's image, and they cannot afford to be anything else but to be a creator, an innovator or an inventor:

Dr. Seyi Oyesola co-invented the "Hospital in a Box." A portable medical equipment that contains surgical and anaesthetic equipment, its operating suite is so compact that it can be air-dropped into inaccessible areas. It is solar-powered and can be set-up within minutes; it serves to bring healthcare and surgery into even the most rural areas of the world. Dr. Oyesola was a doctor, but he knew that being a doctor wasn't enough, he knew he needed to harness his creative potential — a creative potential that the Creator blessed all with — and in doing so, he met the need of many people. Today, he'll no longer be regarded as just a doctor; he's also a creator, an inventor.

Semiconductor technology expert Cyprian Emeka Uzoh holds over 160 patents worldwide; among which is the "electroplated interconnection structures on integrated circuit chips." The New York Intellectual Property Association awarded him as the "Inventor of the Year" in 2006.

Shehu Saleh Balami builds solid fuel rockets, and he builds them here in Nigeria. A graduate of Mechanical Engineering, Shehu didn't let the usual excuses young Nigerians come up with dissuade him from unleashing his creative abilities. Even while living in Kaduna, he built a rocket.

Ndubuisi Ekekwe holds the patent on a microchip that works with minimally invasive surgical robots. He developed chips that control robots that operate on people. Wow! That is an amazing feat!

There are much more examples of people combining their God-given genius ability with hard work. These people have been able to harness their creative capabilities through diligence, and by doing so, they've touched the lives of thousands of people. They have blessed this world with creations, innovations, and inventions. What is your excuse? What are you doing with your creative potential? How many lives have you used your creative ability to impact? Our purpose in this life supersedes being "a good doctor" or "one of the best engineers at my firm." The Creator has put in each of us the ability to be the best at his/her respective fields and then some more; the rest in now up to you — do you want to be exceptional, or you want to remain mired in an ugly average life? In the first seven chapters of this book, we talked about discovering and developing the genius ability within us so that we can be the head in our respective fields, professions, and undertakings. However, you cannot afford to stop at this level; we must all ensure that we deliver every treasure that we have been packaged with by the Creator to our world.

Imagine how much more enjoyable life would be if we all achieve the heights we were made for, imagine how much our country will benefit from your talents. You mustn't waste any more time, the time to discover and fulfil your creative potential is now; the world is waiting for you!

THE DIFFERENCE BETWEEN A GENIUS AND AN INVENTOR

The Merriam-Webster Dictionary defines an inventor as *someone who creates or produces something useful through the use of imagination or of ingenious thinking. It defines an innovator as someone who does something in a new way or someone who effects change.*

According to the definition above, before you can become an inventor, you must have discovered your genius ability. However, that is not the point I'm trying to pass across. The

The creative and innovative power of a Genius

point is — there are millions of people in the world today who have discovered their genius ability but haven't used it to produce something useful. The only way to effect change or create something useful is by taking your genius to the next level; it is by inventing or innovating. Never forget that *all inventors and innovators are geniuses but not all geniuses are innovators, inventors or creators.* If you don't take the necessary leap into creating, you're underutilizing the ability the Creator placed in your life.

Are you familiar with the name Eugene Volokh? Desmond Atkins? Christopher Langan? From a young age, these men tested 200 and above in IQ tests and they could do things as a child that many adults couldn't. They scored perfect scores in exams, they got admitted to colleges before their teenage years, and they graduated with top honours. However, that is how their narrative ends; none of them came up with any ground-breaking invention, none became influential leaders or even wealthy businessmen. All that genius ability and nothing to show for it; instead of using their extraordinary abilities to effect change in the world, they faded away. The world is full of problems and uncertainties, but the world is also full of solutions; the solution is inside my mind, it's inside your mind. Now, we must dig deep and by way of hard work, we must work together in solving the problems around us. It is not enough that you have genius ability or exceptional talent if you don't work hard and use it to impact your community, your nation, and the world at large.

Kim Ung-Yong has an IQ of 210; this gives him more brainpower than the great Albert Einstein and world-renowned physicist, Stephen Hawking. Kim could speak before he was 6 months old, and by the time he was 2 years old, he could read Japanese, Korean, English, and German; a 2-year-old boy! When he was 5-years-old, Kim Ung-Yong amazed the world by solving complex differential equations on live television, and when NASA heard of his exploits, Kim was invited to study in the US. Given what you've read so far, if you were to guess; what would you think Kim Ung-Yong was doing today? An Astronaut? An ingenious Inventor? A genius computer programmer? Well, you would be wrong. As of today, Kim Ung-Yong is an Associate Professor in Shihan University.

With due respect to professors everywhere, Kim Ung-Yong was created for more than being a teacher. This was a man that could speak more languages as a 3-year-old child than many will learn to speak all their lives, he had an IQ 60 points higher than Einstein — one of the greatest scientists of all times. In the end, Kim Ung-Yong didn't make much impact with his gift; he ended up as a nondescript teacher; no creation, invention or innovation registered against his name, even with a 210 IQ!

This isn't an isolated occurrence. History is full of geniuses that didn't live up to their potential; they started excellently but along the way, they fell. It isn't coincidence that most of them fall at the point where they needed to put in more effort; at the point where being a genius was no longer enough; at the point where genius needed to be backed with intensive hard work and dedicated diligence. Either by choice or by ignorance, they have denied the world the benefit of their minds, or the advancement that should have come through them have to wait a while longer. Will you follow their path? Will you let your village, your community, your country and the world, in general, suffer because you lacked the required drive to accomplish what you were created for? It is high time you accepted to transform your life into the reality of what you were born to do; you were created to be a solution provider through your creations, innovations, and inventions.

> *I like being around smart people who are trying to figure out new things. I like the fact that if people really try, they can figure out how to invent things that actually have an impact.*
> BILL GATES

Michael Faraday, who died more than a hundred and forty years ago, is to this day still regarded as one of the most influential scientists in history, and this is a testament to how much he was able to impact the world. Faraday was a prolific innovator, and he always sought to break new grounds and discover new phenomena. Very few people know this, and considering how much he was able to achieve, it is hard to believe, but Michael Faraday had little formal education all his life. As a child, his father wasn't so well-off and from when he was 14-years old, he was an apprentice to the local bookseller. During his apprenticeship, Faraday cultivated the habit of reading and his love for science was inspired by some of the books he read at this time. Just like Bill Gates said in his quote above, Faraday kept himself around smart people by reading books, and by trying to figure out new things; he tried so hard in intensive hard work and he was able to innovate and invent in such a way that left an unusual impact on his generation and even generations yet unborn.

As a result of his interest in science, he attended many free lectures after his apprenticeship at the bookstore and before long, a well-known English chemist took Faraday under his wing. This transformed Faraday's life and with the opportunity he got, he discovered the laws of electromagnets, electrolysis and it was due to his ideas that electricity could be incorporated practically into a useful technology. Faraday also discovered Benzene, an old form of the Bunsen burner amongst many other discoveries. He did so much for science at that time that he was offered a knighthood — he refused it, and till this day, he is commemorated all over England; buildings, schools, streets, and gardens are named after him. For almost 10 years, his picture was on the 20-pound note, and documentaries have been made to shed light on how much he impacted science in his life. Faraday could have been a bookseller, or something else, but once he discovered his interest and love for science, all he wanted to do was come up with new ideas to advance science as the world knew it. He was one of the brightest minds of his time, and he was a chronic innovator.

> *Man's greatness lies in the power of his thought.*
> BLAISE PASCAL

If Faraday could home-school his way to being one of the most influential scientists in the world, what is your excuse? If you are still part of those people who is content with having a good job, earning good pay, and living an average life, you are doing yourself and your world a great injustice. Perhaps, you even had the opportunity of getting a formal education, and all you use your intellect for is to labour for money? Well, I have a message for you today; this is not how the creator planned it, this is not what he created you for. There is no problem with being compensated for your job, the problem is being at your job for a wrong purpose and with the mind-set of a small thinker; Blaise Pascal was correct when he said, as in the quote above, that your greatness lies essentially in the power of your thought — it means if you are thinking small, all you will subscribe to in life is a mediocre life of living for salary but if you are thinking big, you would want to become all the Creator put you on this earth to be, and be living for your purpose as a Creator, inventor or an innovator.

If your job does not give you a chance to broaden your mind and sharpen your intellect, an opportunity to garner knowledge so that you can fulfil your destiny of harnessing the creative ability that we've all been imbued with, then you are in a wrong place in life. It will be very unfair to limit yourself in life because you want to survive; If the creator gave each and every one of us the ability to impact the world, and all you do is work for money, you are no doubt wasting your creative abilities.

What if we all saw the world as an opportunity to meet the needs of others? There are so many needs and problems in our country, and we all have a part to play in creating solutions to these problems, but if you fail to unleash your creative potential, what hope is there for the people who need you, the people whom you have been created to be their savior? If you spend all your days on meaningless toil because of money, when will you be the creator our Creator made you to be?

Can you imagine watching a National Geographic show one day and you see a lion wandering around and looking for food like a scavenger, and almost dying of hunger as if there are no longer animals on earth? With all the strength and power it was blessed with, and with its status as the fiercest predator in the wild; imagine a lion failing to unleash these abilities and instead settle for a beggarly hopeless life. Well, if you spend all your genius ability just scavenging for jobs and salary, and not on activities that do not create any business, art work, invention or innovation for your world, you're wasting your extra-ordinary capabilities like the lion in my illustration. You've been blessed with the ability to be an innovator and a creator; will you rise up to your potential like Faraday did, or will you continue to wallow in a life without true fulfilment? If you sell yourself short and settle for a life beneath your true worth, a life not up to the standard you were created for, you may never find fulfilment in life.

I earlier mentioned Cyprian Emeka Uzoh in this chapter, who has been able to do amazing things with his genius capabilities, but I like to tell you more about him. He graduated from Christ the King College in Onitsha and furthered his education at Rensselaer Polytechnic in New York and the University of Wisconsin-Madison. Today, Cyprian Emeka Uzoh is one of the leading minds in the field of Semiconductor science and technology in the world. He has over 160 patents worldwide — more than 126 in the United States alone — and he is the co-author of almost 40 well-known publications. His inventions have been, and are being used all over the world as we speak, and IBM is among notable corporations that have incorporated Cyprian's inventions in their products.

> *The world is moving so fast these days that the man who says it can't be done is generally interrupted by someone doing it.*
> HENRY EMERSON FOSDICK

Cyprian Emeka Uzoh started like many other bright and intelligent people do with good grades, scholarship opportunities and an undeniably exceptional mind. However, when his peers settle for a 9-4 job, because in their minds, they are saying great things cannot be done, then, as described in the quote of Henry Emerson Fosdick above, those who think great innovations and inventions are impossible will keep on being interrupted by folks like Cyprian, who have understood that the purpose of their genius capability is to create and invent, no matter what the situation is. Cyprian knew he was made for more. Rather than get by with his genius ability in a life lived only for salary, he took it to the next level and unearthed his inventive streak; he just kept on creating and inventing relentlessly. After his first 20-30 inventions, he could have relaxed and enjoyed the rewards of his labor, but he knew better. He knew that a genius that isn't creating is a dormant genius, and as a matter of fact, a useless genius.

Cyprian Emeka Uzoh is a name known in many countries in the world, and when the top minds in his field are called; his name would not be found missing on the list. If he had taken the path that Ibrahim did, he'd probably be working for one of the big corporations, and the world would have been denied the benefits that all his inventions have undoubtedly brought to humanity.

Another Nigerian genius using his ability to create and innovate is Mohammed Bah Abbah. Mohammed created a refrigerating device that works without electricity for people in the rural areas where electric power is either absent or unreliable. His invention won him the Rolex Award for Enterprise, with a prize of $75,000; he used this to produce and distribute his "pot-in-pot refrigerator" to over 10 states in Northern Nigeria. Knowing that the people who needed his invention the most wouldn't be able to afford an expensive product, he produced the device locally and a unit goes for less than 1,000 naira. Because of Mohammad's invention, people in areas without electricity can store their food for 10-14 days without fear of spoilage. What an added value Mohammed gave to the lives of his people! Mohammed saw a need, and he made provisions to meet that need. If more people are like him, imagine how much better things would be for all of us, especially the suffering masses in different nations.

THE WORLD IS FULL OF POTENTIALS FOR DISCOVERIES

When you are an inventor or an innovator, it means you are actively working to discover the treasure of earth, life, and nature. And this can only be done through work. We have so much to discover and so much to be discovered; we have potentials for inventions, potentials for innovations and potentials for discovery all around us. Please be assured that everywhere you go is full of potentials for inventions and innovations. If you look at the trees, for instance, you see potentials for discoveries. When we look at people, we see potentials for innovations. Our lives and the world around us, put together is an innovation and invention laboratory that gives us the opportunity of several amazing discoveries.

How I wish we discover the secrets of these inventions and innovations as a reality, especially in the African continent. This is why I keep reiterating that we need to thank God for work because work is such an amazing invention. Work is a gift from heaven through which we could discover anything and everything that could make our lives better and make us closer to our Creator in a new dimension. This is because when we discover nature, we actually move closer to God. Therefore, WORK is a powerful INSTRUMENT OF DISCOVERY. If you want to make sure that you do not leave this world without coming up with your own discoveries or innovations, you have to adequately understand the concept of work.

It is very possible to have the best and the latest inventions in every area of life if we can just decide to work hard. Imagine if Christians can begin to study, research and begin to work hard in different fields of endeavour, in addition to the help of the Spirit of God, we will surely be an amazement to our world. Just like I have been telling people for some time, I am going to have so many inventions before I die; I am going to have a major invention that is going to influence the whole world. As a matter of fact, I already have an invention that is going to touch every living soul but it is yet to be unveiled. It has not been revealed to the whole world. Being a pastor or a preacher does not stop anyone from delivering your amazing creations and inventions to your generation.

We can all live a beautiful life, a life of constant discoveries and inventions if we can just be dedicated to hard work. Through the concept of work, it is evident that we have been given a blessing by God that we should not live a boring life and that we should not live a life of emptiness. We can enrich the lives of others and enrich our own world through work. Now, I am letting you know that for you to really discover all the beauty and great things God has put in nature, you need work; work is that beautiful instrument God has given us for us not to live a boring life. Every person who has discovered the secret of hard work is a person of discoveries. Believe me — true hard workers don't have an uninteresting life; they are always discovering one thing or the other.

> *And the Lord God took the man, and put him into the garden of Eden to dress it and to keep it.*
> GENESIS 2 V 15

Our destiny as discoverers and innovators was well illustrated by the lives of the first man and woman ever created. There was a process of discovery that began to take place in the Garden of Eden. God gave man an assignment to work in the garden. He knew that through work, they would get to discover life; it was in His design that through work, man would discover nature. This process of discovery began for Adam and Eve — once they were put in the garden as shown in the Bible verse above, one of the things they began to discover was that the ground upon which

The Creative and Innovative Power of a Genius

they were standing and walking could produce herbs and bring forth plants, trees, and fruits. Before they took responsibility to work, nothing grew from the ground. But once they took responsibility, the Bible says "the Lord God made the tree to grow that it was pleasant to the sight and good for food". God began to make everything grow on earth as long as man began to take responsibility. Therefore, their number one discovery was that the earth became an interesting thing. The only reason why the earth became a fascinating thing for man was because they took responsibility. They wanted to know more and understand more, and the more they studied the earth, the greater they discovered their own genius capability. The more they focused on the work God gave them to do, the better they developed the exceptional potentials within them.

Now, it is very important for you to begin to take responsibility for your own sphere of influence. Everybody should be aware that each person has his or her own land of promise. You need to apply these principles I am sharing with you — begin to take responsibility for your own land; begin to take responsibility for that sphere God has called you into. It is time for you to accept responsibility to bring the wisdom and the ingenuity of the kingdom of God to your field; it is time to use your genius potential to restore your nation for God. Many people find it hard to believe that it is by taking responsibility that they begin to discover the precious gems in their land of promise.

Begin to take responsibility by researching and studying your land. Begin to research about the problems of the land; how to solve those problems, and about how similar problems had been solved by the people before you. Once you begin to research into the land of promise you have been called into, you will discover there are more blessings in that land of promise than you have thought or imagined before. You will begin to discover just like Adam and Eve began to discover that the earth was capable of bringing forth trees. They found out that there were things hidden in the earth. Before, it was only God that knew there were seeds embedded in the earth. They initially had no idea that the earth was supposed to be bringing forth trees, herbs, and plants. But once they took responsibility, they began to make new discoveries immediately.

YOU CAN BECOME HONOURABLE

It is the glory of God to conceal a thing: but the honour of kings is to search out a matter.

PROVERBS 25 V 2

The more Adam and Eve discovered that there were things hidden inside the earth, the more curious they became. You need to realize that the same truth applies to your life — there are things hidden in your own earth (promise land) as well, there are treasures hidden in your sphere of influence. There are treasures in every land; the sphere of influence that the Creator has called you into is full of undiscovered reserves. And as the quotation above says, when you make discoveries of things that were once concealed, it is to the glory of God but you also become an honourable person when you are able to do the hard work of searching out hidden treasures.

The creative and innovative power of a Genius

For example, if you are called to the world of medicine, there are so many things to be discovered in this field. I was so shocked when I discovered that when we say somebody is a medical doctor or a doctor of medicine, it's still not an accurate description because there are so many things to discover in the world of medicine alone. If we just decide to consider humanity, we have like seventy billion people on earth today. If everybody becomes a doctor of medicine, we would still not be able to exhaust the field of medicine as a subject of study. Therefore, saying that somebody is doctor or Ph.D. in medicine is impracticable.

Our God is so glorious. And it is amazing how much of an honourable life we can live on this earth. Can you imagine if every medical doctor in the world is made a specialist in just one area of specialization under medicine! They would still not have exhausted what needs to be known about medicine. Whenever you hear somebody say he or she is a doctor of medicine, what you should ask is that 'what area of medicine are they specialized?' Someone could tell you he is a surgeon or a general practitioner. Another person would say she is a gynaecologist. It is only possible to be a doctor in one area of specialization and even in any of such areas, there are just so many things and so much to learn and a lot yet to be discovered. Do you know that if all doctors in the world have been studying gynaecology as a subject, they would not have even gotten to the bottom of that particular field of study?

Today if mankind has been able to figure out everything about the human eye, we would have been manufacturing an artificial eye. Imagine all manner of dentists we have in this world and till today, they still don't know everything about the teeth. There are still a lot of discoveries yet to be made in the area of dental health; if not, when people lose their teeth, they would not be replacing it with a fake one with incomparable functionality. What am I trying to emphasize? There is always something to discover, even in the area of medicine. This is why there is always a place for everybody; you cannot say some people have made all the discoveries there are to be made. That would be a self-deception and a fallacy. We are packaged by our Creator in such a way that there are always things to discover about us.

Every one of us could be discovering things every minute, and we would still not exhaust the wealth of knowledge to be attained. Therefore, through work, you can discover what would make you rich. But you are not just to make money; even the pleasure and the fascination of the discovery of greatness and ability is enough. You cannot be discovering the handiwork of God and be bored. Adam discovered that things can actually spring forth from the earth and that was the beginning of Agriculture. Even in the field of Agriculture today, there are still more to be discovered. Take a moment to imagine the whole world studying agriculture — we would still not have exhausted all the things that could be discovered. There is so much to still discover. Since the days of Adam, the trees were not just growing from the earth they were growing to be pleasant to the eyes, and yet we are still researching this inexhaustible field of study day and night.

Botany is worth considering at this point — the whole botanical world of plants is a science today. There are several universities studying botany and botanical science just because they started making discoveries while observing

The Creative and Innovative Power of a Genius

and studying plants and trees. There is a whole world and a whole science of ecology today just by observing and by studying the relationship of organisms with one another and with other surroundings and environment. Through work, it is very much possible to discover different kinds of food. As a matter of fact, God has shown me how to do inventions and innovations in the area of food production. I am looking forward to a time to gather Christian food scientists and show them how to come up with some of the greatest food technology inventions. As a pastor, I am having an invention in food technology. All of us were created to be inventors and innovators; we only have to use the blessing of work to manifest our glorious destiny.

If you want to be an inventor, you have to meet me one day so I that I can show you ideas on how to invent. I think every human being should have at least one invention. If you can work hard, I can assure you that nature would be a bed of discoveries for you. God has given us a whole world as a laboratory, for exploration but it takes hard work in the library and laboratory of this world; it takes the hard work of adding value to yourself; it takes hard work of creating value in producing some products and rendering some services. It takes intense study, self-analysis, and education through unusual diligence to produce your great innovations and inventions. There is nothing you have chosen to become that you cannot become. I do not believe in failure because all we need to be on top in life is to work hard on nature and work hard on life.

If you have already discovered your genius, then, that is a good news. All you now need to do is to work hard and use your ability to effect change in your country and in the world. If not, your genius isn't fulfilling the Creator's purpose and is essentially useless and of no benefit to humanity. You have been made to see all through this book that you are a genius already; work hard to discover all your talents, develop them, and become one of the greatest inventors or innovators of our time according to the plan of your Creator. In the next chapter, I will be showing you how you can use this same genius ability to create, innovate, and invent your way to wealth.

GOLDEN NUGGETS FROM CHAPTER 8

- In order to find true fulfilment in life, you must do the will of your Creator by making sure you contribute your own creations, inventions, and innovations to your world.

- The life that the Creator has given is much more than mortgaging your life in jobs that will not allow you manifest the all the creative, innovative, and inventive potentials that God has put within you.

- We are all able to create and make new things; but if we do not decide to let this amazing potential within us grow into fruition through intensive hard work, there is no way we will be able to fulfil our destiny of creation of new things.

- The only way you can amount to greatness in life is through work; if your Creator couldn't do it without work, you will be incapacitated, fruitless and unproductive in life without work.

- If you are not known as a creator, an innovator or an inventor on this earth, it simply means you are not totally fulfilling your destiny as a replica or an image of God.

- All inventors and innovators are geniuses but not all geniuses are innovators, inventors

Are you a creator, inventor or an innovator?

or creators. If you don't take the necessary leap into creating, you're underutilizing the ability the Creator placed in your life.

- It is not enough that you have genius ability or exceptional talent if you don't work hard and use it to impact your community, your nation, and the world at large.

- If your job does not give you a chance to broaden your mind and sharpen your intellect, an opportunity to garner knowledge so that you can fulfil your destiny of harnessing the creative ability that we've all been imbued with, then you are in a wrong place in life.

CHAPTER 9

CREATE, INNOVATE AND INVENT YOUR WAY TO WEALTH

Ade looked at the piece of card in his hand and slumped on the wooden bench next to the shop. This was the tenth time he had made a bet on his favorite team and yet they had lost again. How would he survive the following week with just ₦500 left in his account? He swallowed hard to get rid of the lump at the back of his throat as he tried to fight the tears. He had been diligently saving some amount monthly for the past 6 months. In total, he had saved ₦30,000. His friend, Wale, had been betting and had made more than ₦300,000. The amount was what convinced Ade to try his hand at betting as well. As a bright young student at the University of Lagos, he had been commended many times for creating the design of some of the blocks of the new senate building that was undergoing construction. Now, he had lost so much money and his survival was in question.

I shared Ade's story to depict a picture of how badly people want money; most people all around the world are looking for wealth. But they have become blind to the true source of the greatest wealth available to everyone on the surface of the earth. They do not see that the wealth they are looking for in the wrong places is actually abundantly contained inside of them. Friend, my purpose of including this chapter in this book is to show you that all the wealth you will ever need in life is right inside of you. The Creator put you here on earth and already made provision for all the wealth you will ever require in life; this wealth is in no other place but hidden in the genius capability that you already possess inside of you. If you are thinking you are ever going to acquire any significant and lasting form of wealth in life through gambling (as in the case of Ade) or through participating in different pyramid schemes, you are living in self-delusion which is monumentally dangerous to your well-being and destiny on earth.

> *Formal education will make you a living;*
> *self education will make you a fortune.*
> JIM ROHN

Any venture that promises you wealth without the development of the genius capability that is already inside of you is surely leading you on the path of destruction. Now imagine this — was gambling the best way Ade could have used the money he saved for several months? He could have easily invested the money in his future. How? He could have registered for professional courses which could make him a better architect, but he did not know that self-education is potent and lucrative enough to make you a fortune as said by Jim Rohn in the quote above. He could have taken lessons which would open his brain to new ways of creating better designs. The possibilities of wisely making use of his money are endless, but he refused to do that. Like most youths, he was looking for the quickest solution to his financial problems rather than using the creative abilities within him to become better.

> *But you shall remember the Lord your God, for it is He who has given you the power to make wealth...*
> DEUTERONOMY 8 V 18

The Creator has already given you the power to get wealth as affrimed in the verse above. You only need to put yourself in constant remembrance of the work He has already done. He has put creative and innovative tendencies within you so that you will not be living in penury. But if you do not accept your own responsibility of doing the required work, you will be on a path to wasting all your great potentials. If you will ever become truly free from financial struggles in your life, the genius ability within you is the most reliable solution; and the way to go about it is to begin to create, innovate, and invent; when you start creating so much value for the people around you, there is no doubt you will automatically be creating wealth for yourself.

It is quite possible you have wonderful exceptional capabilities within you and still be ignorantly subjected to a life of penury. This was the case of Mr. Flag man, who was born in Ibadan, a peaceful town in Oyo State in 1936. He had a wonderful childhood attending schools in the region of the country where he grew up. The person I am talking about is none other than Taiwo Akinkumi, the man who designed the Nigerian Flag. The flag of a nation represents an idea or an ideal. It is not a mere piece of decoration. It is honored for what it represents. Many flags of different countries are held in high esteem for their history; for the sacrifices made by the people; for the qualities for which the country and people stand. This was why it was such a big deal for the person that would be able to use his genius capability to design this flag to fully represent what a country and a people stand for.

As at when the country was about to be given her independence, people were invited to submit their designs for the new flag of the proposed independent state. The flyers for the competition were posted in many places. Mr. Akinkumi saw one of the flyers in the library and decided to enter the competition. In his own words, he said, *"I took details of what and what is expected to design a flag that would be used by a country that was about to witness the independence. I took part in the competition and my design was selected as the best in the year 1958."* The original design had a star in the middle but when it was time for the final production, the symbol was removed but the colors of the background remained. The green, white, green colour is the creative product and handiwork of Mr. Taiwo Akinkumi.

This man exhibited great talent. He was ingenious and proved to be with extra-ordinary capabilities to produce the best of work among several people that competed for selection of design. But the sad part of the story is that he is currently living in penury. At the early stage of his life, he showed creative tendencies and abilities. Yes, the country honored him then. However, what remains an amazement to me is to know he was expecting the country to honor him forever. Right now, he lives in one of the dilapidated areas in Ibadan and his house is painted the colors of the flag. For the past few years, he has been blaming the Nigerian government for neglecting him and according to him, the government should have monthly allowances for him, and they should take care of his children, and many other things.

> *Creativity is the foundation of wealth...*
> GEORGE GILDER

The bitter truth is that Taiwo Akinkumi definitely discovered his creative tendencies as a young man but he did not convert his creativity for his financial advantage. He did not know that being inventive and innovative is the easiest path to escaping a life of financial slavery. He was ignorant of the truth in George Glider's quote above — that the foundation of wealth is creativity. Rather, he believed the leaders would take care of him because he had done a great service for his nation. Many journalists have interviewed him and he gave accounts on several occasions, of how the country has neglected him for so long.

Friend, let me shock you — majority of those people who feel neglected in life are those that fail to accept the responsibility of using tremendous hard work and diligence to convert the creative abilities and genius potentials within them into creation of wealth — that will make life more comfortable for them and even put smiles on the faces of a lot more people. Instead of living a life that is dependent on others and having needless expectation from government and people, why not take your life into your own hands, and start using every gift and ability God has given you to create the kind of life you want for yourself? If you are not using the talents and the giftings within you, you are inadvertently losing on two sides (a lose-lose situation) —

The creative and innovative power of a Genius

you are wasting the great potentials inside of you and you are making life unnecessarily and extremely difficult for yourself.

The fact that you are a genius does not mean you will automatically become rich. Without working hard in the art of creating, innovating or inventing, you will continue to wallow in poverty, not knowing your laziness is the root cause of all your problems. Wealth does not fall into the laps of geniuses; they work hard to create, innovate, and invent, thereby creating value for other people that will be ready to pay them money for their products and services.

Through the instrument of work, we make our lives richer on a daily basis. By the time you fully understand how to use your genius capability for creative and innovative endeavors, you would begin to enrich yourself and your world daily, materially, mentally, and spiritually. Work is an instrument of discovery; it helps us to discover nature and the wealth that is hidden in nature. If you understand the treasure of hard work, nothing is impossible for you. I already told you the story of how I became a millionaire through hard work. I committed myself to developing the financial genius in me. I studied so hard that I understood all the laws of money. I understood the secrets and principles of profitable investment. I was working with so much creative and innovative tendencies such that I became a millionaire within the space of 9 months. After becoming a millionaire, I decided not to keep it to myself. I used hard work to convert the innovative capability within me to come up with a strategy of how to produce other millionaires. When you understand the principle of work, you will realize that innovations become easy. I found out that it's even easy to produce millionaires and that the same result could be produced everywhere.

If you critically look at your life, you will realize there are things you have done at exceptional levels in the past. Despite this, how well have you committed yourself to the art of creating? You do not have the right to blame anyone else for your financial problems in life. You have only yourself to blame. You can take temporary satisfaction in blaming situations and circumstances but the truth will come to bite you in the face sometime soon.

> *Creativity is thinking up new things.*
> *Innovation is doing new things.*
> THEODORE LEVITT

Everyone is created with creative abilities. If all you do is just use and buy what others are creating, you will not be able to amount to any substantial significance financially. If you look at the lives of people who are wealthy, the common thread in their lives is that they have all been committed to the art of creating, inventing, and innovating. The hard work of creativity and productivity is the secret to their success. To start a business alone involves at least the hard work of creating because it involves thinking up new things that were previously non-existent as Theodore Levitt said in his quote above. And to make a business hugely successful over the years will definitely involve some innovations (doing new things) and possible inventions. I will paint a good picture for you with examples of some of these people who have used their genius, innovative, and inventive capabilities to create an appreciable level of wealth for themselves, their community and their nation:

Mike Adenuga is the founder of Globacom, one of the leading telecommunication operators in Nigeria. Many Nigerians have been dumbfounded at how he came about his wealth and how he rose quickly in the ranks; little did they know that he was called "the Guru" among his friends, a commendation of his remarkable genius ability. It has been said of him that his commitment to work makes him easily adapt to every situation quickly and he has mastered how to handle the transformation of a wonderful idea into an innovation. He is driven by a mindset of doing it better than those who worked on a similar idea before him and he loves excelling the people who are supposed to be more experienced than him. A major secret that culminated in his humongous wealth was that he worked extremely hard at what he knew to be his talent and passion; he creates and innovates using his God-given ability. Friend, I like to let you know that if you are ever going to create a level of wealth that will cause an indisputable impact, you will need to use the force of diligence to cause the genius ability within you to produce great innovations and inventions that will change the story of your nation and even the world.

The state of telecommunications in Nigeria was nothing compared to what it is today before Mike Adenuga became one of the major key players in the industry. He saw an opportunity of adding value to people and to his country through his creative and innovative capabilities. People barely had phones and if they did, the network on the phone was poor such that making or receiving calls could sometimes be a nightmare. Adenuga put in the hard work of obtaining a conditional GSM license in 1999 which was later revoked due to some complications. But great innovators, who will create wealth in their communities and nations do not give up until they achieve their intended results. He continued to give himself to work and he received the second license when the government held another auction in 2003. The consequential result of this was that his telecommunication company spread all around the country and it competitively challenged MTN Network which was the network that somewhat enjoyed monopoly then.

It is crucial to note that the difference between creative or innovative people like Mike Adenuga and the average person who is always complaining about one financial issue or the other is that while an average person keeps complaining about everything, a creative and innovative person defies the adverse circumstance in his environment, goes ahead to believe in the genius capability within, and decides to do all the work it takes to create the desired change he wants to see in his world. The dramatic shift and turnaround caused by the innovations and inventions of creative people is what results in the creation of a substantial level of wealth that an ordinary man only continues to wish or pray for.

No matter how much time you spend in prayer, the kind of wealth that you were created to generate and manage will not fall on your laps if you are not committed to the work of creating, innovating or inventing. According to Forbes, Adenuga's net worth is estimated to be about 6.4 billion U.S. dollars; he did not attain that level of wealth just by wishing; he had to put in the necessary work of adding value to himself and to the continent of Africa. It is almost impossible to find financial giants in this world who are not committed to the art of creating. You have the genius ability within you; all you need to do is to apply it for the work of creation.

The life of Theophilus Yakubu Danjuma, otherwise known as T.Y. Danjuma is worth examining at this juncture. According to Forbes, his net worth is about $1.1 billion, which makes him the fifth richest man in Nigeria. In 1979, at the age of thirty-one, he formed a shipping line known as Nigeria America Line (NAL). The line began business as usual and leased a ship called "Hannatu" which went back and forth Lagos and Brazil. The shipping line became popular and went on to win patronage from other companies in the country. Ever since, the shipping line has continued in business and it is still active till today.

> *Innovation is the specific instrument of entrepreneurship. The act that endows resources with a new capacity to create wealth.*
> PETER DRUCKER

Anyone who is serious about creating wealth does not rest on his oars; such people keep on making use of the exceptional abilities resident within them to keep meeting needs, solving problems, and adding value to people's lives. They understand the words in the quote of Peter Drucker above, that innovation is one of the most instrumental factors that endows people with a greater capacity to create wealth from resources. This was why one shipping line was not enough for Danjuma, the business tycoon. In 1984, he decided to establish COMET Shipping Agencies Nigeria Ltd which is now one of the largest independent agents that currently operates in Nigeria. As if that was not enough, General Danjuma kept on using his creative abilities and decided to branch into the oil and gas industry. He established South Atlantic Petroleum Limited (SAPETRO) which is an oil exploration and production company. Yet, some people keep sitting idle and make their major business the criticism of what everybody else including the government is doing wrong; but the ironic part of their life is that they fail to criticize themselves; they fail to see that they are leaving a great wealth of resources in terms of potentials and talents within them untapped and they keep looking for answers where there is none. Friend, refuse to be the mentally blind person who already possesses an enormous amount of wealth within him but does not realize that without the process of conversion through immersion in hard work, all the wealth possessed will not be beneficial to him or anyone else.

ACTIVATING YOUR CREATIVE GENIUS ABILITY FOR FINANCIAL GROWTH

Ben kicked angrily at the stone in front of him and howled in pain. He was frustrated and nothing was going his way, and now, even his toes hurt from kicking the stone. He smiled sadly at the irony of it all; he kicked at the stone to let off some steam and he ended up adding to his troubles. He considered his life as he limped home, he was poor and he had no way of improving his condition anytime soon. After graduating from the university about three years ago, he had been unable to nail down a job. Studying computer engineering had sounded attractive to him when he was applying for admission and he had believed he would get a

THE CREATIVE AND INNOVATIVE POWER OF A GENIUS

well-paying job within months of graduation, that turned out to be wishful thinking on his part, and years later, he was still waiting for his dream job. On getting home, he turned on his laptop and started watching one of the various movies he spent the night downloading. As he watched the movies, he mused dreamily, "if only someone could gift me millions of naira. Wouldn't that be amazing"?

> *I am a great believer in luck, and I find the harder I work, the luckier I get.*
> THOMAS JEFFERSON

How many times have you been caught in such fantasies too? Hoping and wishing that things would get better when you can do something more proactive about your condition. Many people have silent expectations. They wish for many good things; they wish for good jobs, they wish for financial buoyancy, they wish for some lucky break. However, all they do is to wish. In Thomas Jefferson's word of wisdom, the only way to guarantee more luck, if that is what you want is to work harder. In Ben's case, rather than spend his days watching movies and wishing for luck, why couldn't he use that time to think up ways he could apply the knowledge he garnered while in school to do something profitable? Elon Musk started in a similar manner. However, he didn't spend his days hoping and wishing, he was actively looking for ways to make himself luckier through hard work rather than lie in wait for it. He was activating the creative genius within him for his financial growth.

> *There is no doubt that creativity is the most important human resource of all.*
> MARGARET J. WHEATLEY

Your creativity is a very important resource, what are you using it for? Are you using your ability for anything tangible; financial or otherwise? What do you spend your time on? Is your genius being wasted or are you creating and inventing? You need to face the fact that being a genius can only be maximized with hard work and you will not be able to reach your full potential in life without creating, inventing and innovating. Many people in the world today work from 8 am to 5 pm every day. Most of these people are basically laborers and quite a few of them live for jobs that can barely meet their most basic needs. It is painful to see, so many people, with a wide array of genius potentials, settling for a life of mediocrity. They live this way because they have failed to apply the genius ability they have to create and innovate. They failed to realize that only through creating, innovating, and inventing can genius ability be used to bring wealth and financial independence. Think about it, if you have discovered your genius ability but you refuse to be creative, what separates you from those who haven't tapped into their ingenuity? What is the point of discovering your genius if you'll end up as a manual laborer, a man that lives to consume and never create?

You get to see a lot of people who are so preoccupied with consuming. They see a new invention, probably shipped from another country, and all they want to do is own it. For example, if you carry out a survey, you would be surprised at how many people desire the latest iPhone or Samsung product. The ironic part of it all is; everybody wants to use the latest gadgets but virtually nobody is thinking about creating an equivalent. There are thousands of computer and phone engineers in our country but it is hard to see people applying their abilities in order to come up with a product to rival these brands. What most people think about is how to own the best, few people are thinking about being the best.

Have you heard of the brand called 'Tecno'? Tecno produces affordable and good quality phones and tablets for the masses. The brand is very popular in developing nations because of their business model, in fact, they are seen as a rival to other popular brands such as Samsung, LG, HTC, and so on. What is their model? It's quite simple actually; they make devices that strike the perfect balance between quality and affordability, so much so that virtually everybody can afford a 'Tecno', and the performance levels are high enough to rival that of the more expensive brands.

This brilliant idea was birthed by the innovative mind of Nnamdi Ezeigbo. Ezeigbo looked at the technology market and searched for a way to break the stranglehold that famous brands had on the market, he noticed that prevailing phone brand in the country was Nokia and many people could not afford it. Why not create something that could be easily affordable for everyone? With an idea in mind, he made moves to implement it. Nnamdi went to China and partnered with a man who worked for a company called Bird. Together, they created the first Tecno phone for sale in Nigeria. As of today, Tecno has gained popularity not only in Nigeria, the brand has infiltrated countries like Kenya, Egypt, Ethiopia, and many more. Ezeigbo applied his innovative ability, he saw an opportunity and he took advantage of it. What is stopping you from doing the same? You have the ability in you to create and innovate; you need to begin to harness that ability. Stop sitting around wishing for luck when you can make yourself the luckiest person on earth through hard work.

> *Wealth is the product of man's capacity to think.*
> AYN RAND

Wealth doesn't come to those who wait for it, it answers to people's dedication to the production of goods and services. Use your creative ability to innovate your way to a life of financial accomplishment. Whether or not you acquire wealth depends on how much you can apply your genius ability. And the process of applying your genius ability usually starts with thinking. As affirmed by Ayn Rand's quote above, every form of wealth that humans have been able to produce have originated from the hard work of thinking.

What about something that we experience every day? Think of this for a moment: you're lying down on your bed, working on your laptop. You can hear the faint sounds of the television in the background. You are so engrossed in your work that you barely notice you have had constant power supply for about two hours. All of a sudden, power goes off. You groan and shake your head because it is a usual occurrence. Within the space of five minutes, the neighborhood is buzzing with the sounds of numerous generators rescuing their owners from the boredom of a dark night. Yes, generators have been very useful in our day to day lives. They

The Creative and Innovative Power of a Genius

help us cope with the incessant power outages and when your generator is on, it's like power was never seized. As good as generators are, the world is generally far advanced beyond this and there are better technologies that are more environmentally friendly. These technologies are available all over the world for uninterrupted power supply. Why is it that we do not have enough people who will rise up and accept to use the genius potentials in them to create lasting solutions to these problems? There is no difference between people who are using their creativity to create wealth and you. The best form of resources are available to everyone; it is only diligent and hard workers who take advantage of opportunities. Start creating, start innovating, most of all, start thinking critically about how you can use your genius ability to enrich yourself and your world.

You can become super rich and wealthy by creating and inventing. For being the very first person to invent something new, it has the potential of bringing a lot of financial fortune your way. Look around you, this country is practically bursting with resources with only few people taking advantage of the opportunities they present. We have so many natural resources in the country yet we unreasonably import many things. Let me give you a few examples of the ridiculous things we import in this country. Do you know how useful a toothpick is? Do you also know that many acres of land in the country are filled with trees? Despite being this blessed, we still import toothpick! It is quite bizarre that something this trivial cannot be produced in the country. It is even more absurd that the country spends about $1.5 million importing toothpicks every year.

CREATE, INNOVATE AND INVENT YOUR WAY TO WEALTH

To leave you in even greater shock is the fact that we import something as ridiculous as pencils. No, you did not read that wrong. Pencils are still being bought from other countries till today. It begs the question of what is so hard about making pencils. Recently, a newspaper report stated that Nigeria will start producing its's own pencils by the end of the year 2018. That is still quite far and will not happen if there is no commitment to actually start doing the work to get it done.

As simple as candle is, it is still being imported into the country. It is something that could easily be manufactured in Nigeria, yet, we still ask foreign countries to sell candles to us when we could have used the money for something else. If someone decides to start creating candles today, the kind of wealth possible for such a person will be unimaginable. Becoming financially rich is not rocket science; all you need to do is to apply yourself to the necessary work of research and innovating. Simply look at what the society needs and go ahead to create it. Wealth is not a phantom concept, it is well within your reach, all you have to do is apply your creative genius.

All these examples go to show that there are lots of opportunities for wealth in our dear country. The only reason why we have so many people complaining about poverty is because they fail to apply their genius ability to creating, innovating and inventing. They find it easier to blame the government or somebody else for their financial situations. They neglect the fact that the very opportunities that will make them rich are all around them. Rather than apply themselves, they sit and wish for good fortune. Nnamdi Ezeigbo did not get his ideas out of the blue, he worked so hard for it. He studied the market and saw what was lacking, he made use of his innovative genius. What was the end result? He amassed wealth not only for himself, but for generations to come. If you understand the principle of hard work and diligence in pursuing your goals, you will never be living in cluelessness anymore; you will always be drenched and soaked with new ideas.

FROM SMALL BEGINNINGS COME GREAT THINGS

Alex had just completed the mandatory National Youth Service Corps and she was desperately looking for a job. Most of her friends had tied down lucrative jobs but she remained jobless. Just two days earlier, her best friend had called her that she just got her employment letter from a multinational corporation. Alex was happy for her, but it only served as a reminder of her own woes of unemployment.

She had been told she had a natural gift for designing and drawing, "but who has that ever helped," she grumbled inwardly. She had tried using her talent to secure some tasks but she wanted more than that out of life, she wanted a well-paying job. She braced herself and brought out her phone, and started scrolling through her contacts. It was time for her uncles and aunties to be "useful". They knew people who worked in very good companies that could give her the lucrative job she'd always wanted. She summoned courage and called a few of them. After almost an hour on the phone, she didn't get any encouraging responses. She shut her phone and went to sleep.

Create, Innovate and Invent Your Way to Wealth

> *Don't wait for something big to occur. Start where you are, with what you have, and that will always lead you into something greater.*
>
> MARY MANIN MORRISSEY
> (AUTHOR OF "BUILDING YOUR FIELD OF DREAMS")

Looking at Alex's life critically, what would you say she's doing wrong? What would you do differently if you were in her shoes? With so many people telling her she had a natural talent for art, she should have persisted and developed her talent to a level when she cannot be ignored. If she had, it would certainly have been better than what she was doing currently; which was nothing. She wrongly assumed that her talent couldn't do anything to help her situation, she forgot that all great things start small. Rather than start with what she had and build it up, she sat, waiting for a well-paying job. Any wise person will heed the words in Mary Morrissey's quote above — you do not have to wait for something big to occur; start where you are with what you have, and if you do not give up, your life will end up becoming great. No matter how developed your talent or ability is, if you refuse to apply it creatively, innovatively or inventively, it will remain dormant.

If you are looking for a good example of a man willing to start small and apply his innovative genius, a personality you should not forget about is Aliko Dangote. Dangote started his business at a very young age. At that time, there were many big companies trading in the same products, but he didn't let that dissuade him. He had innovative new ideas that soon made him a force to reckon with in the sugar business. He started with having just a sugar shop to producing sugar on an industrial scale. Afterwards, he didn't give up, he continued growing and he expanded his business to include flour, rice, cement and many other ventures.

> *Small opportunities are often the beginning of great enterprises.*
> DEMOSTHENES (GREEK STATESMAN AND ORATOR OF ANCIENT ATHENS)

Today, he is in charge of one of the biggest corporations in Africa, but he started small. He is not only the biggest producer of sugar in Nigeria, he is also the largest producer of all the products he makes. Because of his inventive abilities, he is now the richest man in Nigeria, even Africa. He had genius business skills and he didn't mind starting small. He knew the beginnings are of little consequence, he knew all great companies started small and he believed that he could build something great as long as he continued innovating and creating. In the end, he was proven right. Poverty is not a strictly physical scarcity problem; it is largely due to mental passiveness. Poverty starts mentally before it progresses to the physical. The very minute you stop utilizing and tasking your brain to be creative and innovative, you become poor.

Having read Dangote and Akinkumi's stories, can you see how their different statuses in life were determined by how diligently and consistently creative one was compared to the other? Do not make the same mistake Akinkumi made so that you will not look back years later, thinking of all the brilliant ways you could have made a difference but you refused to. Do not live the rest of your life in penury because you failed to use your genius ability to innovate and invent. Ignore your smallness of your beginning and strive to use your talent to make a difference.

Another billionaire that started from humble beginnings was Elon Musk. When he graduated from college, Musk never depended on or waited for a white collar job. Straight from college, he built his first company Zip2. After some years, he sold it and built another one, a company that eventually became PayPal. On and on, Musk kept growing and growing. Today, he owns about 4 companies and is worth in excess of $11 billion. He knew he had a talent and he used it to propel himself to a life of financial buoyancy. He didn't care about getting a fat paycheck like many of his mates, the only thing he was aiming for was just to create by doing what he loves doing. The truth is that very few young people today plan to use the genius ability imbued in them to create companies that will challenge these multinationals, and this way of thinking is preventing them from reaching their peak financially. They believe the quicker and easier way is better than the creative, innovative way. In reality, it is not.

Now that you have read these people's stories, what is your opinion? What do you want to spend your time doing? Do you still want to be watching movies daily or you want to spend your time creating? You cannot afford to keep complaining and wishing for a miracle breakthrough in life. It is high time you deliberately begin to take your life into your own hands, and chart the course of your life. Prosperity is what you desire and need; all you have to do is to use your creative abilities to get what you want. Stop doubting your genius potential. Create something; test it, and continue to add value to your world. That is your surest path to becoming wealthy.

Economic recession is a major problem many people put their focus on instead of creating solutions. The irresponsibility of the people of a nation is the principal cause of economic recession. When all people do is to get engrossed in consumption, and not actively involved in production process, depression and recession are usually the consequences. Instead of being the one complaining about every situation, be one of those people that simply go about their way working hard in the process of creating, innovating, and inventing? If you choose the latter, your money problems will definitely come to an end and you will experience prosperity beyond your imagination.

Now you know the truth; you have no excuse to remain poor. You have gained a thorough understanding of the blessing of the genius ability that the Creator has put within you. Continue to create, innovate and invent to live a prosperous life and make our nation prosperous. In the next chapter, I will be showing you a powerful force that will let loose amazing creative and innovative abilities within you.

GOLDEN NUGGETS
FROM CHAPTER 9

- The Creator put you here on earth and already made provision for all the wealth you will ever require in life; this wealth is in no other place but hidden in the genius capability that you already possess inside of you.

- If you are thinking you are ever going to acquire any significant and lasting form of wealth in life through gambling (as in the case of Ade) or through participating in different pyramid schemes, you are living in self-delusion which is monumentally dangerous to your well-being and destiny on earth.

- Majority of those people who feel neglected in life are those that fail to accept responsibility of using tremendous hard work and diligence to convert the creative abilities and genius potentials within them into creation of wealth.

- If you are not using the talents and the giftings within you, you are inadvertently losing on two sides — you are wasting the great potentials inside of you and you are making life unnecessarily and extremely difficult for yourself.

- Wealth does not fall on the laps of geniuses; they work hard to create, innovate, and invent, thereby creating value for other people that will be ready to pay them money for their products and services.

- If you are ever going to create a level of wealth that will cause an indisputable impact, you will need to use the force of diligence to cause the genius ability within you to produce great innovations and inventions that will change the story of your nation and even the world.

- Great innovators, who will create wealth in their communities and nations do not give up until they achieve their intended results.

- While an average person keeps complaining about everything, a creative and innovative person defies the adverse circumstance in his environment, goes ahead to believe in the genius capability within, and decides to do all the work it takes to create a desired change he wants to see in his world.

- Refuse to be the mentally blind person who already possesses an enormous amount of wealth within him but does not realize that without the process of conversion through immersion in hard work, all the wealth possessed will not be beneficial to him or anyone else.

- What most people think about is how to own the best, few people are thinking about being the best.

- Wealth doesn't come to those who wait for it, it answers to people's dedication to production of goods and services. Use your creative ability to innovate your way to a life of financial accomplishment.

- The best form of resources are available to everyone; it is only diligent and hard workers who take advantage of opportunities. Start creating, start innovating, most of all, start thinking critically on how you can use your genius ability to enrich yourself and your world.

- Becoming financially rich is not a rocket science; all you need to do is to apply yourself to the necessary work of research and innovating. Simply look at what the society needs and go ahead to create it. Wealth is not a phantom concept, it is well within your reach, all you have to do is apply your creative genius.

- If you understand the principle of hard work and diligence in pursuing your goals, you will never be living in cluelessness anymore; you will always be drenched and soaked with new ideas.

- You do not have to wait for something big to occur; start where you are with what you have, and if you do not give up, your life will end up becoming great.

- Poverty is not a strictly physical scarcity problem; it is largely due to mental passiveness. The very minute you stop utilizing and tasking your brain to be creative and innovative, you become poor.

- Do not live the rest of your life in penury because you failed to use your genius ability to innovate and invent. Ignore the smallness of your beginning and strive to use your talent to make a difference.

- When all people do is to get engrossed in consumption, and not actively involved in production process, depression and recession are usually the consequences.

CHAPTER 10

INTELLECTUAL CURIOSITY OF AN INVENTOR/ INNOVATOR

> *Without curiosity, there will never be innovation.*
> STEVE STOUTE

Most of the greatest inventions, from the early age flint stone, down to the global iPads, have been the product of human curiosity. These have not been due to some miraculous and divine interventions, or a random occurrence of nature that cannot be explained, but these have been products of human efforts in intensive hard work, immersed in extra-ordinary curiosity and sheer determination. Steve Stoute's quote above puts it well — nobody should even dream of innovating or inventing if he does not have an extreme level of curiosity.

Can you imagine that even the founding of a Nation came as a result of curiosity? America, that is seen as a great nation today would not have been discovered if it was not due to the fearless curiosity of Christopher Columbus. His curiosity did not allow him to stay in one place waiting for

THE CREATIVE AND INNOVATIVE POWER OF A GENIUS

a miracle to happen or waiting for an idea to come through the vision of the night. He went after what he desired with a curiosity that was strong enough to result in WORK that will birth the creation of a soon-to-be world power.

Do not make a mistake — the curiosity I am talking about here is not the same as wishful thinking or day dreaming. I am talking about curiosity of the diligent mind that is looking for answers. Any great discovery, creation, invention and innovation made or produced on this earth came out of curiosity. The great treasures from nature, mineral resources like coal, petroleum, gold, diamond, and all manner of rare natural resources were discovered as a result of high level of curiosity.

> *Be curious always! For knowledge will not acquire you; you must acquire it.*
> SUDIE BLACK

The reason why you have not made many discoveries in life is because you have not been curious enough. As Sudie Black said, you probably have been waiting for knowledge to acquire you; you should realize that it is through an unusual curiosity you acquire real knowledge when everybody else keeps wallowing in the darkness of ignorance. Columbus was so curious that he badly wanted to discover the New World. He wanted to trade spices in India but instead landed up in the Americas. He mistook it for India and thought that the tribesmen who welcomed him were Indians. He called them Red Indians since they were brightly dressed. If it were not for Columbus's curiosity, there is a little chance that America would not have been discovered till now, or would have been discovered much later that she would not be the great nation that she is today.

> *I am neither clever nor especially gifted. I am only very, very curious.*
> ALBERT EINSTEIN

When discoveries are well applied, they lead to the greatness of the discoverer; it is the level of your discovered and applied discoveries in life that will determine your level of relevance. Even the great Albert Einstein (who has often been quoted in this book because there is just too much to learn from him), as shown in the quote above, once acknowledged that if you remove his curiosity from him, then you would realize that he is neither gifted nor clever.

The greatness of a nation that we see today started with a discovery by a single man and his name will never be forgotten in the history of America. Let me ask you a question — What discoveries will you make that will stamp your name to the sand of history? I am certain you do not want to live your life and end up as a nonentity. The truth you need to know is that you will only make great discoveries if your curiosity is high enough to spur you to the hard work that separates the gracefully diligent from the common man.

Every truly curious person is a natural hard-worker; because until a particular thirst for knowledge or answers is quenched by discoveries, he or she does not rest from his or her quest. Columbus was curious enough to be travelling from place to place in search of answers. He was not going to stay at his comfort zone until he achieved undeniable relevance with his life. Life is full of problems and challenges; only people who provide solutions are truly relevant in the affairs of men.

> *Without curiosity, all doors remain closed.*
> MEHMET MURAT ILDAN (TURKISH PLAYWRIGHT AND NOVELIST)

How do you know a man who is ready to start changing his world with innovative and inventive ideas? Such people are not difficult to recognize — they are simply busy with the work of providing solutions to the problems that have been begging for answers for years. They will not rest until they see certain substantial, dynamic and definite shifts they have been longing to see in this world. And the thing that keeps pushing them is their high level of curiosity; they know (just as in Mehmet Murat Ildan's quote above) that without curiosity, all doors will remain close for them. One of the principal keys that open up your door to greatness is curiosity; through a highly diligent curiosity, you unlock the treasure of the genius capability within you and you get to impact your nation, and your world in an unusual way.

At this point, I like you to ponder on the following questions — What will it be like if many people get curious enough, to actively and purposefully start searching for answers to the long-lasting electric power supply problem in our dear country? How great will it be if many youths and young adults are curious enough to provide answers that will rescue nations in Africa from the drowning effect of the flood of corruption and ineptitude that is ravaging her economy? Many African nations will definitely

Intellectual curiosity of an inventor/innovator

not be where they are today if a lot more people have engaged their curiosity for conversion into highly productive and life-changing endeavors. Instead, a lot of people are busy with mindless religious activities while some others are busy trying hard to impress the people that do not care about them with their latest gadgets, wears, cars, and other mundane things of life. Your pre-occupation is a major determinant factor that tells if you will arrive at your pre-destination in life or not.

Do you look at your life, and you cannot see much of unique creations? Do you feel that your life is more or less like an impoverished desert without useful innovations; a life rife with lack of wonderful ideas? I think I know what the problem might be — there is an extremely high probability that you are suffering from one of the most common limitations of the ordinary man — low level of curiosity.

Without a doubt, lack of curiosity simply means acceptance of a status quo; it means the situation of things are just okay enough for you that you are not in any way moved to start asking questions and doing the work of improvement and development that will change the condition of things for the better. One of the most dangerous and self-defeating things that can happen to you in life is for you to live without curiosity. If you are wondering why I said this, I made this statement because there are always more than enough reasons to be curious, and if anyone cannot see them, the person may be blind without knowing.

For example, If people are still crying in this world, it means somebody needs to be curious enough to start working to stop their sorrows; if poverty, sicknesses, and diseases are still killing people in different parts of the world, it means we need many more people to be curious enough to make discoveries, innovations and inventions that will solve these problems. Manoj Bhargava's curiosity led to him realizing some of the issues that plague billions of people. He wants to tackle problems facing these people, and he has earmarked a substantial part of his financial net worth to doing so. The Indian-born American billionaire saw how important water is to the world, and how some people suffer from a lack of it, and as of right now, he is working on a machine that takes saltwater from the sea and refines it to clean drinkable water. This man is not a young boy that is still in his thirties, yet he is still working hard to make a difference. The fact that your age is already above 50 years does not mean you can still not make a difference in your generation. You can always start from where you are in the diligence and hard work of your curiosity to make sure you add value to the lives of as many people as possible before you leave this world.

Manoj Bhargava, who has claimed his life is all about the impact he can make in this world, especially the suffering nations and the poor masses came up with the invention called the Rainmaker, which is a desalination machine that is capable of distilling salt water into freshwater, and a single unit can provide water for a small town. With thousands of units in production, Bhargava may have found a way to make sure that nobody suffers from drought ever again. Bhargava has also invented, and is working on the production of a hybrid bicycle that generates electricity. With this invention, all you have to do is paddle for one hour, and by doing so, you would have generated clean and pollution-free electricity for 24 hours. No monthly costs or anything, just paddle and enjoy unlimited power. Wow! What a great way to convert one's curiosity and love for humanity!

Let me bring something else to your attention — Lack of curiosity is the breeding ground for complacency because it encourages resistance to changes. And in case you don't know, complacency is the worst enemy of innovation and invention. Curiosity makes you live in the world of ceaseless inspiration, which in turn gives birth to unusual insights. When you are full of Insight, then you will be soaked and drenched with amazing ideas. When you mix hard work with your creative ideas, what results is a deluge of inventions, creations and innovations. This is the surest way to ascertain that the genius capability you were created with is not wasted; it is the way to ensure that you are fulfilling your purpose.

Consider it to be an abnormal thing if you find out that you are hardly curious about anything. The Creator originally created us to be very curious; that is why we had little or no knowledge when we were born a baby. He created us to find answers to the questions and problems of life. The kind of curiosity that a baby exudes is what should be a dominant inherent characteristic of every adult. How do we want to make discoveries, create, innovate, and invent if we have lost the great virtue of curiosity that we were packaged with at birth? You are a wonderfully created and awesome package from God but you will not discover how precious you are, how much of a great value and worth you are if you are not hardworking and curious enough. This pristine, God-given energy, called curiosity is the force that has led most of the great innovators and inventors of all times to impact this world in such a profound manner.

Anyone who is naturally curious is always at work in search of knowledge; curious people are always researching and experimenting, asking questions because they want to find out what, why, and how of what is generally not discernible or accessible to the ordinary mind. Curious people work very hard to use their findings of what already exists in nature or the work that has already been done by somebody else to creatively produce new innovations and inventions.

THE CURIOSITY OF ISAAC NEWTON

We have talked about Isaac Newton in previous chapters but he is worth mentioning here again — He was so curious to an extent that he was busy thinking and trying to get an answer to why an apple fell downwards towards the ground rather than going upwards towards heaven. He engaged in the hard work of productive thinking and he did an intensive research; he spent sleepless nights in his room and finally, after a well-above-average level of work and rigorous scientific research, he came up with his theory of gravitational force. There is an undue vacuum that you are leaving behind in this world if you do not bless the world with your own discoveries; there are gaps that need to be filled with your own innovations and inventiveness. If your focus in this world is largely on consumptiveness and not on creativity, you will never be able to make the maximum impact you were created to make.

Are you still having sleepless nights because of your personal domestic challenges? If Newton was a worrier about daily survival and was not thinking about solving a problem that will answer the question of every human being

Intellectual curiosity of an inventor/innovator

alive at that time, including the ones yet to be born, how do you think his name will still be of extreme relevance today (many years after his death)? Being preoccupied with the mundane things of life — what to eat and what to wear, the car to ride, and the house to live — will not get you to any height of notable significance in life. No matter how hard you think you are working, if it is majorly geared towards your daily survival, your chances of being an innovator or an inventor is extremely slim. Until you begin to think big, you will not be able to do big things. Thinking small is thinking just about yourself; while thinking big is being preoccupied with solving the problems of your Nation and the world at large.

CURIOSITY MEETS NEEDS AND SOLVES PROBLEMS

Curiosity is born out of need, and need is the mother of inventions. Newton had a need — the need to find out why an apple would fall vertically and hit his head. He took it as a personal responsibility to find out the reason why that was so; he was not waiting for someone else to do it. Can I ask you this — How responsible have you been in this life? How responsible have you been in solving the problems of your nation? If you are just thinking about your personal needs, and not the needs of many other people, there is no way for the creativity that you were packaged with from heaven to develop to a useful treasure that attracts the attention of the world. Without accepting responsibility to solve the problems you were created to solve by coming up with great innovations and inventions, your life will keep running as a waste of a most valuable resource. You already have what it takes to do this; the genius capability is within you waiting for the day of manifestation.

There is a proverbial locust and cankerworm that is eating up the destinies of many people in third world nations. Ask me what that is — Dependency on others or government to solve problems for them. Waiting on the government to solve every single problem the masses are complaining about is an outright display of irresponsibility. And the lack of a responsible mindset is what leads to a life that is devoid of curiosity and deserted of amazing creations, innovations, and inventions.

Benjamin Franklin was curious as to what powered lightning; he believed it was electricity and he wanted to validate his curiosity/thoughts by doing further research on the idea. This led to his kite experiments and subsequent discovery that lightning was indeed electricity. If Franklin hadn't been curious enough, or inventive enough to act on his curiosity, the world may be without electricity today.

> *Curiosity is one of the permanent and certain characteristics of a vigorous intellect.*
> SAMUEL JOHNSON

My friend, how many questions do you have on your mind that you are actively working towards getting answers for? Nobody becomes great without answering some unanswered questions of life; everybody showers accolades on renowned Innovators and Inventors because they do the hard work of solving the questions that have plagued mankind for decades. For example, in 2003, Russian math

Intellectual curiosity of an inventor/innovator

genius Grigory Perelman solved the Poincare conjecture, a mathematical theorem that had been unsolvable for more than 100 years. When he was nominated for the Fields Medal — the math equivalent of the Nobel Prize — Perelman rejected the Medal and the million-dollar payout that comes with it. He said the knowledge he acquired while proving the conjecture was more important to him that any prize. What a man! As Samuel Johnson said, curiosity is one of the permanent and certain characteristics of a vigorous intellect; if your intellect would be extremely great and vigorous, it is only going to happen through curiosity; Perelman rejected the gift of one million dollars because his curiosity was much more important to him than money. His life is a proof of the greatness that can come from not living one's life for mundane things of this world.

Alexander Fleming had a burning curiosity to defeat germs, and this led to his discovery of penicillin. When Louis Pasteur lost 3 of his children to typhoid, his curiosity about the disease was piqued. This led to his invention of the pasteurization process to ensure that no other father will mourn the death of his kids. The telephone that we all enjoy today also came from the curiosity of another inventor — Alexander Graham Bell wanted to know more about signals and how they worked; his research led to the first telephone prototype in 1876. His curiosity also led to his creating the photo phone, a better version of the phonograph among many other inventions.

What have you been doing with your life? How curious have you been about finding out what it takes to create a positive change in your community and in your nation? You were created to be a creator, innovator, and an inventor but if you have exchanged your curiosity for the need for survival and pleasures of life, you are doing a great injustice to your destiny; you are doing an enormous disservice to your world.

For example, I like to discover people, I like to understand people. Because I love people and I love God, I am always curious to find ways of serving them, of ministering to them and help them. I get so intellectually curious that I begin to fill myself with wisdom. This is why each and every of my messages you listen to is a new discovery. I found out that life is full of discoveries if anyone will engage the habit of intellectual curiosity. Hard work in curiosity is the instrumentality and the secret code for all of us to live an exciting life. This is because your life will be full of amazing fun and excitement if you are constantly making new discoveries.

> *And a river went out of Eden to water the garden, and from thence it was parted, and became into four heads. The name of the first is Pison: that is it which compasseth the whole land of Havilah, where there is gold; And the gold of that land is good: there is bdellium and the onyx stone. And the name of the second river is Gihon: the same is it that compasseth the whole land of Ethiopia. And the name of the third river is Hiddekel: that is it which goeth toward the east of Assyria. And the fourth river is Euphrates.*
> GENESIS 2 V 10 — 15

Intellectual curiosity of an inventor/innovator

One of the greatest treasure that the first man and woman (Adam and Eve) had in the Garden of Eden was curiosity. Like I told you before, they discovered the treasures that come from the trees; then they discovered the ones that come from the ground. After discovering the earth, they kept on working until they discovered the rivers (as seen in the passage above) and what could be done with the rivers. Gold was first discovered by man in the Garden of Eden; if they were not intellectually curious, they wouldn't find it.

They discovered that water could be segregated when their curiosity led them to see where the water was parted in four different directions. Now, science has now made it easy for us to separate water from land and as humans, we are now able to do our own artificial lakes, and have our own pools. We are now well able to control water and this is another whole world of discovery that originated in the Garden of Eden. Yet we are all still studying about water and we have not fully understood it and that is why water is still sinking and killing people. Friend, please realize that space is full of discoveries but it is only intellectually curious people who find them. Everywhere around you can be a world of discovery; but for that to be true in your life, you must love to work hard and do it unapologetically.

When I meet with Christian scientists sometimes soon, I am going to tell them the discoveries that are hidden in passages of scriptures; and the inventions that can be produced from this particular passage. Christians go to church and they are doing religion when we are supposed to be taught how to thoroughly read the bible and be able to understand and see what ordinary people cannot see. After reading the Bible, we should be able to come up with ideas because every beautiful thing you see on this earth started with an idea.

I like to teach people how to discover, just by reading the bible that it is possible to do amazing things with your life, when every area of the Bible you read lets you tune into the mind of the spirit of God and into the wisdom of people that came before you. When you read the passage of the scriptures, you should be making a discovery for yourself; it is a definite rule that people who engage in the hard work of curiosity end up in wonderful discoveries. If you have discovered your own calling in life, it is even easier. You can focus on your calling, and work very hard in your sphere of influence so that you don't just live a life of vanity. For you to be remembered for time and eternity, you must add some value to humanity and intellectual curiosity will go a long way in helping you. However, I like to let you know that the greatest discovery is about God. In addition to discovering nature and discovering yourself, invest yourself in discovering God, and then you become a revelator of God's regeneration, a reflection of His glory and of His nature.

THE CURIOSITY OF LEONARDO DA VINCI

While he lived, Leonardo da Vinci was always different from everyone around him; he thought different, his ideas were different and his paintings and drawings reflected an imagination beyond the world he lived in at that time. Da Vinci was in a different class entirely from the inventors of his time and the quality of his works showed a distinct superiority. His designs were futuristic and while designing some of his contraptions, he included components that were not yet invented or produced. He had an unprecedented understanding of human beings and nature, and this helped him to understand the human mind like no one else could. He modified the technological conventions of his time and many of his designs are still in use today. The people around him hardly understood many of the things he conceived, but that didn't stop them from being impressed with his works.

Giorgio Vasari, Leonardo's biographer once said of him, "*The gifts that Leonardo possessed seemed unlimited, standing to all areas of human knowledge and skill — artist, scientist, anatomist, sculptor, botanist, architect, musician, engineer, inventor, entertainer, and philosopher.*" However, Leonardo had a singular flaw; as brilliant as he was, he found languages difficult. What he lacked in translation, he made up for with a keen observatory an analytical mind. It is a fruitless exercise to keep worrying about the abilities you see in others but lacking in you. Have you found out the ones inbuilt inside of you waiting for discoveries? Leonardo knew his strength and he maximized his opportunities in such profoundly and dynamically amazing ways than has probably been witnessed or recorded in all books of history.

He had an avid curiosity and the state of his environment did little to limit him; his curiosity and his creativity combined to make him one of the most prolific inventors the world has ever seen, and in his life time, he built some technological marvels. Most people relate the name Leonardo da Vinci to art, but he contributed a lot to science and technology as we know it. He did insightful research in optics, anatomy, hydrodynamics, and mechanical engineering among many others. He designed with painstaking detail the design of the military tank, a helicopter, a double-hulled catamaran, a calculator and so on. In his time, he didn't have the raw material necessary to build these devices, but the designs he left behind were so detailed that people were still making use of his designs long after he was gone.

Da Vinci set a very high standard for himself and he threw out most of his paintings because he deemed them not good enough; only 15 survived. Along with these paintings, he left almost 1300 pages of drawings, designs, and jottings. These give us a peek into the mindset of one of greatest inventors the world has ever seen. He might have been a great artist also, but the reason his art was so unique was because of da Vinci's deep interest and curiosity in science; he was curious about what made everything around him tick, and when he couldn't understand it from a technological standpoint, he resorted to the hard work of dissecting it diagrammatically and the diligence of drawing the body with great detail. The level of attention you pay to details while doing your work or while researching shows how much industrious and hardworking you are in using your curiosity and energy to provide solutions to the problems found around you. One of the major secrets of great people in life is that while the lazy man hardly observes changes around him or in his work, the great people are devoted to the diligence of paying careful attention even to seemingly minor details related to their work or calling.

Da Vinci saw everything — including the human body — as a machine and he sought to understand how it functioned; he used strings to replace muscles while investigating how they worked with bones, which he represented with levers, he also designed the first humanoid robot, "The

Intellectual curiosity of an inventor/innovator

Robot Knight." All these seemed weird to people who were around him, but it laid some groundwork for understanding anatomy for latter generations.

"Curiosità" is an Italian word for a voraciously curious approach to life; a hunger to keep learning about yourself and everything around you. It entails asking questions of yourself and pursuing knowledge no matter what restrictions life puts in your path. Da Vinci was of the belief that all things in the world are interconnected and when the connection isn't known, it isn't a sign that there is no connection; rather, it is a sign that more research must be done to find the connection.

Da Vinci was passionately curious about everything he saw and he regarded everything as a creative challenge. Vasari once said about him,

> *Men of genius sometimes accomplish most when they work least, for they are thinking out inventions and forming in their minds the perfect ideas which they subsequently express and reproduce with their hands.*
> GIORGIO VASARI

Though, hard work and diligence have been specially emphasized in this book. But as in Vasari's quote above, you must learn to differentiate smart hard work from the busyness of ignorant people. You may not see men of great accomplishments sometimes physically busy, but they are in the diligence of their minds, thinking out inventions and forming the ideas they will soon be working on into perfection before they embark on it. Seventy-five percent of all great and wonderful accomplishments is first achieved in one's mind (and translated into writings, drawings, plans, and notes) before embarking on physical activities.

> *The future belongs to the curious. The ones who are not afraid to try it, explore it, poke at it, question it and turn it inside out.*
> LOVELLE DRACHMAN

Leonardo's curiosity was so great, it was never sated with assumptions, he wanted to do thorough work on everything, and until he cracked the puzzle that plagued him, Da Vinci would keep at it for years if needed. As a result, his notebook was littered with incomplete notes and random drawings. Da Vinci was constantly questioning, observing and trying to unlock the secrets of the present. He believed that there was a connection between the present and the future, and the only way to unlock the secrets the future held was to understand the present beyond any doubt. Think about it — Leonardo Da' Vinci who was gone since more than a century ago is still relevant in our world today. Indeed, the future belongs to the curious!

How does curiosity help creativity? Well, the world as we know it is constantly changing and before we wrap our heads around an impressive new technology, another even more impressive technology is being discovered. To be able to keep up and make an impact in this ever-changing world, you must first have an understanding of how everything works, and without being unrelentingly curious, the complexity of the world may continue to evade you. It is definitely always more productive to ask why than to ask how; and using the hard work of your curiosity to gain an innate

Intellectual curiosity of an inventor/innovator

knowledge of the context within which a problem exists make solving the problem easier.

Steve Jobs was one of the biggest names in the tech industry, and he wasn't tech savvy; how is that? The answer is simple; Jobs was curious about the people around him, and he always sought what made them tick. This gave him a better understanding of what people wanted, and he was able to satisfy their wants and needs without having to ask them personally. Unlike most, he didn't let the fact that he wasn't a tech genius prevent him from succeeding in that niche. Instead, he utilized one of the most important keys to creativity; diligent curiosity about everyone and everything around him, and through this, he was able to leave his name in the sand of history.

You have been able to gain from this chapter one of the major keys to your innovativeness and inventiveness. To unlock your creative genius, you must first utilize the power of curiosity in deliberate diligence and hard work. If you're not really curious, you will never come up with something new. In the next chapter, I will be showing you how to make your curiosity even work better, and how to maximize the energy of your creativity in order to bless the world in an unusual way.

GOLDEN NUGGETS
FROM CHAPTER 10

- Nobody should even dream of innovating or inventing if he does not have an extreme level of curiosity.

- It is through an unusual curiosity you acquire real knowledge when everybody else keeps wallowing in the darkness of ignorance.

- When discoveries are well applied, they lead to the greatness of the discoverer; it is the level of your discovered and applied discoveries in life that will determine your level of relevance.

- You will only make great discoveries if your curiosity is high enough to spur you to the hard work that separates the gracefully diligent from the common man.

- Life is full of problems and challenges; only people who provide solutions are truly relevant in the affairs of men.

- Through a highly diligent curiosity, you unlock the treasure of the genius capability within you and you get to impact your nation, and your world in an unusual way.

- Lack of curiosity simply means acceptance of a status quo; it means the situation of things are just

Intellectual curiosity of an inventor/innovator

okay enough for you that you are not in any way moved to start asking questions and doing the work of improvement and development that will change the condition of things for the better.

- You can always start from where you are in the diligence and hard work of your curiosity to make sure you add value to the lives of as many people as possible before you leave this world.

- Curiosity makes you live in the world of ceaseless inspiration, which in turn gives birth to unusual insights. When you are full of Insight, then you will be soaked and drenched with amazing ideas.

- If your focus in this world is largely on consumptiveness and not on creativity, you will never be able to make the maximum impact you were created to make.

- Nobody becomes great without answering some unanswered questions of life; everybody showers accolades on renowned Innovators and Inventors because they do the hard work of solving the questions that have plagued mankind for decades.

- You were created to be a creator, innovator, and an inventor but if you have exchanged your curiosity for the need for survival and pleasures of life, you are doing a great injustice to your destiny; you are doing an enormous disservice to your world.

- It is a fruitless exercise to keep worrying about the abilities you see in others but lacking in you. Find out the ones inbuilt inside of you waiting for discoveries.

- The level of attention you pay to details while doing your work or while researching shows how industrious and hardworking you are in using your curiosity and energy to provide solutions to the problems found around you.

- One of the major secrets of great people in life is that while the lazy man hardly observes changes around him or in his work, the great people are devoted to the diligence of paying careful attention even to seemingly minor details related to their work or calling.

- To be able to keep up and make an impact in this ever-changing world, you must first have an understanding of how everything works, and without being unrelentingly curious, the complexity of the world may continue to evade you.

CHAPTER 11

THE SOLITUDE SECRET OF AN INVENTOR/ INNOVATOR

Nikola Tesla, the father of modern-day electricity was regarded in some circles as a mad scientist when he was growing up. He could solve differential and integral equations by heart from when he was a child, he gambled away his tuition when he was in the Austrian Polytechnic in Graz, and when he was 22-years old, he cut ties with his family and moved to another country. It is, therefore, strange that someone with such erratic behavior could come up with the incredible inventions that Tesla did. Apart from the outstanding work he did on the alternating current (AC) electricity supply, Tesla also made extraordinary contributions to the fields of electromagnetism and wireless radio communications; in fact, his work with radio communication is still in use till today.

I started here with Nikola Tesla; but we have looked deeply into the lives of extra-ordinary people all through this book; people who discovered their genius capability and committed themselves to the art of using their great potentials to create, innovate and invent in unusual ways. There is an attribute that is very crucial that we may be missing in the lives of these great people; a common but scarcely understood secret they all took advantage of, to convert their hard work into amazing accomplishments, and this secret is no other one than the secret of solitude which will be explored all through this chapter.

Therefore, Tesla is a good example to begin with, in order to vividly depict the power of solitude. He was a man who had numerous vices that ailed him but grew up to be one of the most prolific inventors of his time. But how was he able to do this? The answer is in his quote below. He knew how to make his mind so sharp and keen by secluding it from outside influence in order to unleash his extra-ordinary creative abilities.

> *The mind is sharper and keener in seclusion and uninterrupted solitude. Originality thrives in seclusion free of outside influence beating upon us, to cripple the creative mind. Be alone — that is the secret of invention: be alone, that is when ideas are born.*
> NIKOLA TESLA

You can literally sense this man's understanding of the power of solitude even in his quote. He strongly emphasized it: "*...Be alone, that is the secret of inventions; be alone, that is when ideas are born.*" If you ever hope to come up with great inventions in life; if you ever hope to give birth to ideas that will shake your generation and generations yet unborn, you cannot afford to turn a deaf ear to the counsel of someone like Tesla; he attributed all his greatness that we are still celebrating till today to the habit of solitude. Friend, solitude indeed is the secret you need

The Solitude Secret of an Inventor/Innovator

to be disciplined and hardworking enough to exercise, in order to bless your world with all the amazing inventions and innovations hidden inside of you.

> *Without great solitude, no serious work is possible.*
> PICASSO

Even as a teenager in the Austrian Polytechnic, Tesla was a loner; he was said to work form 3 a.m. until 11 p.m., with no regard for weekends or holidays; all he wanted to do was study electricity and come up with unprecedented ideas and theories. Even when he severed ties with his relatives and moved to another country, he didn't seem to mind; Tesla was a man used to his own company. He didn't see solitude as a disadvantage or something to agonize about, rather, he made productive use of his time alone, and he hardly sought the company of others; he viewed it as a waste of time that could be used doing more important things. He had a focus and he worked towards it, which he did best in seclusion. He knew that without great solitude, no serious work is possible, as positively affirmed in Picasso's quote above.

Tesla realized that he was most effective when he was alone and he made a decision to bask in his solitude and use his time alone to harness his creative genius. He would lock himself in his laboratory for hours — days even; he wouldn't see anyone, talk to anyone, and he only left the laboratory to eat and nap. As a result, Nikola Tesla was able to come up with so many beautiful innovations and inventions.

The Creative and Innovative Power of a Genius

> *Language has created the word 'solitude' to express the glory of being alone.*
> PAUL TILLICH

What do you think of solitude? Being in solitude is not the same thing as being lonely. Just as Paul Tillich said, the word 'solitude' is used positively in language to express the glory of being alone; it is simply a deliberate effort to separate yourself from unnecessary human influence and environmental distractions. There is no amazing creation without solitude and there can be no major earth-shaking invention made in an environment that is full of distractions. If you truly desire to unleash your creative or innovative genius, then you must be prepared to cut out the irrelevancies in your life. Like Tesla's story shows, hard work is important, but the environment in which you work is equally as important.

> *The best thinking has been done in solitude...*
> THOMAS EDISON

Take a moment and reflect on this; assume that as you're reading this book, you have been interrupted many times by, say your phone; will your chain of thoughts be the same as someone else reading it with no distraction? Now, apply this logic to something more mentally tasking like coming up with your inventions and innovations, how will you ever be able to gather your thoughts together and discover the creative genius in you if you live your life mired in endless distractions? As Thomas Edison affirms in his quote,

The Solitude Secret of an Inventor/Innovator

the best form of thinking you will ever do can only be done in solitude.

What if Tesla had gotten carried away by inconsequential things, what would the world look like today without his inventions? By not seeking the solitude you need to unleash your creative genius, you're starving your nation of the benefits that should have come from you, and through you to mankind. It is very crucial that you begin to do the hard work of running away from outside interferences and abrupt interruptions to your thought-flow if you want to ever leave a mark on your generation. Spend time in solitude, this is the only way to discover your inventive genius, it is the only way you can add value to the world with ground-breaking innovations and inventions.

Now it is time to tell you about another legend whose good advice put him in trouble! In the early 20th century when continuous planting of cotton was destroying farmlands of good yield, George Washington Carver advised farmers in his area to try crop rotation, growing peanuts alongside the usual cotton; he told them about the nutritional value of peanuts and how it could help save their depleting farmlands. After some consideration, they took to his advice and surprisingly, it worked. Within a few years, their lands were more nutritious than ever before and they had more cotton than they could imagine. However, because peanuts where virtually unknown at that time, they didn't know what to do with all the peanuts they harvested. Before long, their storehouses were stinking from the wasting and rotting peanuts.

The Creative and Innovative Power of a Genius

Carver's supervisor, Booker T. Washington told him about the problem. He was fearful that due to the highly volatile nature of race relations in, some of the white farmers would not hesitate to retaliate on the bad advice of Carver — a black scientist. Obviously expecting Carver to be as worried as he was, Washington was surprised that Carver took the situation calmly. The quizzical look on his mentor's face must have compelled Carver to explain the inner workings of his mind. He told his boss about benefits he derived from solitude.

Born into slavery, Carver was a sickly child who could not go to work with other slaves in the field. This necessitated his being left at home most of his childhood days to assist in the garden. That was when he developed a love for plants of every variation; trees, herbs, vegetable, etc., Carver loved them all. His love for Agriculture was what made him choose to study it even further when he got older.

> *The more powerful and original a mind, the more it will incline towards the religion of solitude.*
> **ALDOUS HUXLEY**

When faced with the peanut problem, Carver was not worried because he had such a powerful and an original mind; and as Aldous Huxley describes the characteristic of a man with such kind of a powerful mind, Carver perfectly knew how to incline towards the religion of his solitude. He told his boss, *"All my life, I have risen regularly at four in the morning to go into the woods and talk with God. When everybody else is asleep, I hear God best and learn my plan... this morning I asked Him why He made the peanut."*

The Solitude Secret of an Inventor/Innovator

Booker thought his friend was losing his mind, but he let him continue. Carver went on, *"He told me: separate the peanut into water, fats, oils, gums, resins, sugars, starches, and amino acids, and combine these under my three laws of compatibility, temperature and pressure, then you will know why I made the peanut!"*

Booker laughed hard at the incredulity of Carver's claims and, he asked sarcastically if God always gave Carver the right answers. Carver answered with a wry smile, *"Let me put it this way: The Lord always provides me with life changing ideas. Not that I am special. The Lord provides everyone with life changing ideas. These ideas are quite literally a treasure from the Almighty. It is up to each of us, however, to choose and dig for the treasure."*

There are very important lessons to learn from the legend's words above; the first one is that the Creator has provided every one of us with ideas that will change our lives and the lives of everyone around us; it is up to us to dig for the treasure of those ideas. The second lesson is: the only way to hear the voice of the Creator — to unleash the creative genius we've all been blessed with — is when we are in solitude. Why didn't Carver hear the voice when he's in the marketplace? Or when he's out with friends? The answer is simple; the best condition for digging up the treasure in us is when we're free from worldly distractions.

> *The monotony and solitude of a quiet life stimulates the creative mind.*
> ALBERT EINSTEIN

The Creative and Innovative Power of a Genius

George later went to his laboratory and stayed there for a whole week because he knew how to practice the wisdom in the quote from Albert Einstein; he creatively utilized the monotony and solitude of a quiet life such that when he emerged, he'd developed several new products that could be produced from peanuts. He introduced this to the public in a series of simple brochures, and just like that, the market for peanuts skyrocketed! Today, George Washington Carver is credited with saving the agricultural economy of the rural south. In the end, he developed about 300 products made entirely from peanuts. One trip to that special place in the woods, and Carver came up with an idea that averted racial tensions and fundamentally changed the agricultural industry forever. That man was just incredible!

Carver (just like Tesla) discovered the secret of harnessing ones' inventive and innovative genius and he used it to unleash his abilities and impact the world. You can also sacrifice some hours of chit-chat with friends, watching television, browsing the internet, talking on the phone, partying, and so on to separate yourself in solitude; and through it, you get to discover the treasure the Creator has put in every one of us. It takes a diligent mind to get into solitude in order to add value to the world; I implore you to engage this secret to bless your world with your creations, inventions, and innovations instead of continually wallowing in the life of distractions that keep others in an average or an ordinary life.

THE IMPORTANCE OF TRANQUILITY TO CREATIVITY

Jide's day began like it always did — with an alarm blaring in his ears. He touched 'snooze' in an attempt to steal 10 extra minutes of sleep but after what seemed to him like a minute, the alarm sounded again, "What?" he exclaimed, "ten minutes went by so quickly?" He rubbed his eyes groggily and got out of bed. He still felt very sleepy, but he couldn't afford to stay longer in bed; if he takes too much time to get ready and leave his house he'll be caught in rush hour traffic. Twenty-eight minutes after he woke, he was on his way to work. He tuned in and listened to the news, while at the same time checking his messages. About 15 minutes from his office, there was a minor accident and he had to wait for almost 30 minutes before the road was cleared.

By the time he got to work, he was slightly late, but luckily for him, many of his co-workers were also delayed by the commotion on the road. As he was settling in to finish the work he was doing from the previous day, his boss called him. "How's the assignment I gave you coming along?" "I'm about 80% done, I was just about to finish it when you called," Jide answered. "Well, make sure you've completed it before you go to lunch, we're presenting it to some board members immediately after lunch." Beads of sweat formed on Jide's brows; To Jide, that only meant one thing; he would have to miss his lunch break to complete the task and get it ready for presentation.

The presentation went well, and he got compliments from around the table. He was in high spirits as he walked back to his office, as he entered, Samson — one of his co-workers — was waiting for him. When Jide saw him, his spirits plummeted; he had forgotten all about the promise he made to put Samson through some things. By the time they were through, it was closing hours. As he made his way to his car, Jide realized he hadn't eaten anything all day; he decided to get some food on his way home. Some minutes after he left the restaurant, he got stuck in traffic. He sighed in exasperation and unwrapped his food; he was too hungry to wait till he got home. Just as he was about to turn into his street, he remembered he had to pick up his laundry, he backed his car up and went back the way he came.

When he unlocked the door to his apartment, he felt relief beyond measure. He collapsed into a nearby sofa and loosened his tie. He checked his phone and replied some messages and a few calls and before long, he dozed off right on the sofa. Jide was awoken by the sound of his alarm, once again signaling the beginning of another day just like the one before — he didn't even make it to his bed.

> *The more tranquil a man becomes, the greater is his success, his influence, his power for good. Calmness of mind is one of the beautiful jewels of wisdom.*
> JAMES ALLEN

Jide's life as described above is similar to the life of millions of people all over the world. Many people live in the face of so much chaos that it isn't surprising that very few people are able to productively utilize their creative or inventive genius. Take Jide for example, when will he be able to find the tranquility he needs to be creative? How can he find some solitude in his frenzied life? His weekends will mostly be for catching up on the hours of sleep he missed during the week, then he'll visit his friends and relatives, maybe even go to church and so on. So, even if Jide had an incredible creative ability, without the tranquility necessary to harness it, how will his ability be of benefit to those around him? Even if the Creator had placed in Jide an ability that would help our country — or the world — one way or another, where/when will he find the solitude needed to dig up that treasure? James Allen puts it well in his quote; he said the more success, influence, and greatness you want to achieve in life, the more tranquil you need to become. No man is truly wise until he understands the necessity of calmness of the human mind. If your soul never finds calmness, it is simply and practically impossible that you will be able to produce any meaningful invention or innovation.

If your life is just as hectic — maybe even more so — than Jide's, then you must know that a drastic change is needed in your life. It takes a deliberate attempt to give your life the tranquility that is needed in order to be fruitful in life. However, it is important to note that this kind of tranquility we are addressing here has more to do with your mental state than the physical state; you can be extremely busy, yet live your life in calmness. You may be in the face of great tribulation, yet still find enough solitude to unearth your creative genius.

The Creative and Innovative Power of a Genius

> *I go through a long period of gestation before I'm even ready to write, and I consider the process of gestation just as important as when you're actually sitting down, putting words to the paper.*
> — WOLE SOYINKA

Wole Soyinka was imprisoned for roughly 22 months, but because he knew how important tranquility was to creativity, he didn't — like many others would — dwell on his surrounding and his predicament, instead, he used the time spent in isolation to top-up his creative juices. Because he wrote about the injustices of the government during the civil war, he was accused of supporting the Biafrans and subsequently jailed. Knowing how influential Soyinka was, and how he could still send missives out even while in prison, they made sure he wouldn't have access to pen and paper. Yet, this great genius managed to author numerous poems and notes. He must have used those 22 months for gestation as he said in his quote above. He understood the importance of solitude to creativity, and while prison would have incapacitated some people, he decided to convert it into a period of gestation in tranquility. Whenever you understand that the best output of your life comes out of solitude in addition to your soul being in a tranquil state, you will never take it for granted anymore; any opportunity you have to deliberately go into solitude or whenever you are forcefully put into one will be maximally utilized. Why not apply this simple secret and begin to touch your world with unusual creations, innovations and inventions!

From when Soyinka was a young man, he would go far away from his home to meditate and seek inspiration. He loved nature and he is said to have discovered some beautiful natural sites in his search for tranquility and solitude. There was a particular guava tree he loved so much, for the cool shade it afforded him and how tranquil being under it made him feel. Wole Soyinka's curiosity, imagination, and zest for learning were his motivating forces, and solitude and calm helped him become the creative genius the world knows him to be today.

> *I am a glutton for tranquility.*
> WOLE SOYINKA

Take a moment to think about this again — a man was unjustly imprisoned but refused to dwell on his difficult situation; he refused to feel lonely or helpless like many others in the same situation would have been. Instead, he decided to convert that situation to his benefit and the profit of others. Despite the fact that he was deprived of writing materials while in prison, he still found a way to write with his mind; only gluttons for tranquility would attempt a feat like that. As soon as he was released from prison, he published a collection of poetry titled 'Poems from Prison'.

Now, I need to ask you — What have you been using your own prison experience to do? Are you sitting down, crying in a pity party about how bad, life has treated you or you are willing to use the force of tranquility that your prison offers you to elevate yourself from the prison to the palace? You need to realize that even if you are not forcefully put in prison, you need to regularly create your own 'solitude' prison (whether in your house or in any quiet and calm place) to lock yourself in for the release of unusual

The Creative and Innovative Power of a Genius

creativity. Solitude is not a choice if you ever want to come out with the great and amazing creations and inventions that God has put inside of you.

I hope you have noticed the clear difference between the lifestyles of Jide and Soyinka. Just like over 90 percent of the people in the world, Jide has been caught up in the rat-race of life; all he cares about is to make ends meet without seeking to tap into whatever ability he has been blessed with; too many activities rendered him totally blind to the power of solitude. Just imagine that Soyinka also lived that kind of life rife with extremely busy day, full of self-inflicted must-do events and activities, how many people would have known his name today? He would have become absolutely lost in the rat race of life that most people are ignorantly and perpetually trapped in. He would have gone to the grave with such great and marvelous works he was able to eventually bless his world with. Friend, you need to know that running to and fro or up and down will not necessarily bring you any significance in life. It is being in an environment that is tranquil enough, being in your treasure of solitude that you can consciously bring out all the inventions and innovations that are destined to make you a great person on earth.

People like Jide will always find an excuse as to why they haven't tapped into the treasure we've all been blessed with. "My job is too hectic, I hardly even have enough time for myself," "I have a lot on my plate; solitude is for people without responsibility" and so on; not knowing that they are consciously throwing away what is able to transform them into some of the most highly valued and sought after persons on earth. If your life has been taken over by mundane things; so much so that you can't take a break from it at all, to find out your true purpose, you need to do a self-reassessment and a personal re-evaluation of your life. Without solitude, you will never be able to convert all the wonderful treasure inside of you to be of tangible value and immense benefit to this world.

THE BEST PLACE TO WORK IS IN SOLITUDE

> *Most inventors and engineers I've met are like me ... they live in their heads. They're almost like artists. In fact, the very best of them are artists. And artists work best alone... I'm going to give some advice that might be hard to take. That advice is: Work alone...*
> STEVE WOZNIAK

In the mid to late 70s, Steve Wozniak was of the opinion that the world would be a better place if everyone had a user-friendly personal computer, and he was determined to build such a computer. At that time, such an idea seemed incredulous because the computers around were as big as minivans and were so pricey, individuals could hardly afford them. He took some inspiration from the work of the simpatico band of engineers, the Homebrew Computer Club and started working on his dream. He was said to work on the design in solitude for about 3 months nonstop, and in the end, he and Steve Jobs started one of the biggest technology companies in the world today, Apple. The desktop computer and the laptops you see everywhere around today are as a result of Wozniak making use of solitude to

The Creative and Innovative Power of a Genius

create something that is of extreme benefit to the whole world. Steve sounded his advice so loudly and convincingly in his quote about the best place or way to work if you are a creator or an inventor — work alone!

If you ever hope to develop your genius ability and tap into your inventiveness to such an extent that will let you make an unusual difference in your world, it is highly imperative that you seek out some solitude, for it is only in solitude that a man sees things with utmost clarity and have a deeper understanding of himself and everything around him. So many people go through life without ever being alone with their thoughts, and from childhood through adulthood, they live a life characterized by chaos and distraction. You have to take control of your life; after all, it is your life. It is high time you disconnect yourself from unnecessary media, to rid yourself of all the things that deprive you of the solitude you need to flourish. Wozniak knew he needed to be alone to birth his innovation, and he withdrew from the hustle-bustle of the world to get it done. Is it your phone? Is it the internet? Or your friends? For you to unearth your own creation or invention, you must develop your own solitude habits, and enroll yourself into the league of extra-ordinary people.

> *When I am, as it were, completely by myself, entirely alone, and of good cheer — say, travelling in a carriage or walking after a good meal or during the night when I cannot sleep — it is on such occasions, that my ideas flow best and most abundantly.*
> **Wolfgang Mozart.**

The Solitude Secret of an Inventor/Innovator

Now let me tell you about Wolfgang Mozart, who started playing musical instruments at age 3. He was a musical prodigy, who could read music notes before he could write. He was first taught how to play piano by his father but he later taught himself how to play the violin, trumpet, and clarinet. Mozart wrote about 600 works of music before his death and is among the most enduringly popular of classical composers. His music was featured in more than 300 films. Many of his works were acknowledged as pinnacles of symphonic, concert ante, chamber, piano, operatic and choral music. The secret of his creativity, however, lies in his quote above. He was able to recognize the moments and the places where he got the best of his music ideas. These were all times of solitude when he was alone by himself. He said it could be while travelling alone, walking after a good meal or in the middle of the night. You need to find out what works best for you, but I can guarantee you that your best creative moments would always be when you are in solitude.

No one has made any notable invention while watching television, or browsing social media or while chatting aimlessly with friends. It is said that the creators of most social media platforms are not really social; in fact, some of them seek seclusion to turn their idea into something tangible, and when it does, they make billions of dollars off their work. Why would you allow that same social media to prevent you from discovering your own invention? Mozart created beautiful music and he did it by tapping into the creative genius that was in him. We all have one unique ability or another but without being immersed in the hard work of solitude, we may never discover it talk less of utilizing it.

Another person who understood the great importance of solitude is Albert Einstein, who is regarded as the father of modern physics and one of the most influential scientists and intellectuals of all time. Einstein's writings laid the foundation of modern physics and changed views on space, time, mass and energy. He provided empirical evidence for the atomic theory, enabled the determination of Avogadro's number and therefore, the size of molecules. Einstein solved the riddle of the photoelectric effect and proposed the special theory of relativity. In a nutshell, and as already mentioned in a previous chapter, if the word genius as we know were to be given a face, it will be the face of Albert Einstein.

> *...although I have a regular work schedule, I take time to go for long walks on the beach so that I can listen to what is going on inside my head. If my work isn't going well, I lie down in the middle of a workday and gaze at the ceiling while I listen and visualize what goes on in my imagination.*
> ALBERT EINSTEIN

Einstein was a man that enjoyed solitude from when he was a young man. He was so self-engrossed that on occasions, he'd forget the names of people close to him; even in the presence of other people, Einstein would withdraw into the recesses of his mind. He loved sailing because it was one of the few ways he could be truly alone. On his 50th birthday, he was given a boat as a gift, only he had to

The Solitude Secret of an Inventor/Innovator

be constantly rescued from the sea. He enjoyed his solitude so much that he'd get distracted and get lost sailing at the sea. Einstein recognized how much he needed solitude to get in touch with the genius that lied deep in his mind. As he said in his quote above, he usually took time to go for long walks on the beach because he wanted to listen to what is inside his head; he would lie down in the middle of the day and gaze at the ceiling to be able to accurately visualize his imagination. No wonder he was able to touch the world in an outstanding way through his theory of relativity and other discoveries. He knew that he had all the answers to his questions and all he had to do was simply eschew the distractions of the world and reach deep within him. In the end, Einstein shed light on many of the scientific problems of his time, and his inventions remain relevant till date.

Do you also know that the solution to all the problems of the world can be found in your mind? Do you believe that the Creator has placed in every one of us the capacity to create something that will be beneficial to the whole world? If all these great men believed that the way to tap into the bottomless resource of the genius of our minds is through solitude, what are you waiting for? They did not only preach about the importance of solitude, they showed us how effective solitude and tranquility is through their creations and their inventions. What I'm telling you right now is; you have within you the ability to be an Einstein or a Mozart. The important question you now need to answer is; do you want to be enlisted in the hall of fame of renowned geniuses, creators, innovators and inventors? If you do, then you must emulate the lives of the great men discussed in this chapter and embrace solitude in order to profoundly impact your world with great results of your, creations, inventions and innovations. In the next chapter, I will be showing you yet another highly important quality of every great inventor and innovator.

GOLDEN NUGGETS
FROM CHAPTER 11

- Solitude indeed is the secret you need to be disciplined and hardworking enough to exercise, in order to bless your world with all the amazing inventions and innovations hidden inside of you.

- There is no amazing creation without solitude and there can be no major earth-shaking invention made in an environment that is full of distractions.

- The Creator has provided every one of us with ideas that will change our lives and the lives of everyone around us; it is up to us to dig for the treasure of those ideas.

- The only way to hear the voice of the Creator in order to unleash the creative genius we've all been blessed with is when we are in solitude. The best condition for digging up the treasure in us is when we're free from worldly distractions.

- No man is truly wise until he understands the necessity of calmness of the human mind. If your soul never finds calmness, it is simply and practically impossible that you will be able to produce any meaningful invention or innovation.

- You need to regularly create your own 'solitude' prison (whether in your house or in any quiet and calm place) to lock yourself in for the release of unusual creativity. Solitude is not a choice if you ever want to come out with the great and amazing creations and inventions that God has put inside of you.

- Running to and fro or up and down will not necessarily bring you any significance in life. It is being in an environment that is tranquil enough, being in your treasure of solitude that you can consciously bring out all the inventions and innovations that are destined to make you a great person on earth.

- If your life has been taken over by mundane things; so much so that you can't take a break from it at all, to find out your true purpose, you need to do a self-reassessment and a personal re-evaluation of your life. Without solitude, you will never be able to convert all the wonderful treasure inside of you to be of tangible value and immense benefit to this world.

- It is only in solitude that a man sees things with utmost clarity and has a deeper understanding of himself and everything around him.

- No one has made any notable invention while watching television, or browsing social media or while chatting aimlessly with friends. The creators of most social media platforms are not really social; in fact, some of them seek seclusion to turn their idea into something tangible, and when it does, they make billions of dollars off their work.

CHAPTER 12

THE FERVENT TENACITY OF AN INVENTOR/ INNOVATOR

If you have read this insightful book up to this point, you must have realized how innovators change things; how they take new ideas, sometimes their own, sometimes other people's, and develop and promote those ideas until they become an accepted part of daily life. As you were already hinted in previous chapters, the fact of life is that these inventions and innovations do not come on a very easy or common platform; they come on the grounds of dogged diligence. Therefore in this chapter, I will be showing you why ground-breaking inventions and innovations require a relentless tenacity of a goal-getter and a history maker to bring unusual creations from the intangible realm of the mind to the visible and tangible physical world.

Inventions and innovations require self-confidence, a taste for taking risks, leadership ability and a vision of what the future should be. One may have all these characteristics, but it takes years to develop all of them fully to the level that they begin to yield the intended results. And this is the truth — It takes tenacity and relentlessness for these characteristics to eventually transform to innovativeness and inventiveness.

TENACITY OF HENRY FORD

Henry Ford did not invent the automobile. He didn't even invent the assembly line. But more than any other single individual, he was responsible for transforming the automobile from an invention of unknown utility into an innovation that profoundly shaped the 20th century and continues to affect our lives today.

Henry Ford's beginnings were perfectly ordinary. He was born on his father's farm in what is now Dearborn, Michigan on July 30, 1863. Early on Ford demonstrated some of the characteristics that would make him successful, powerful, and famous. He organized other boys to build rudimentary water wheels and steam engines. He learned about full-sized steam engines by becoming friends with the men who ran them. He taught himself to fix watches, and used the watches as textbooks to learn the rudiments of machine design. Thus, young Ford demonstrated mechanical ability, a facility for leadership, and a preference for learning by trial-and-error. These virtues would become the foundation of his whole career.

Ford began to show his tenacity early in life when he could have followed in his father's footpaths and become a farmer. But young Henry was enthralled by machines and was willing to take risks to pursue that fascination. He eventually left his father's farm to become an apprentice at the Michigan Car Company, a manufacturer of railroad cars in Detroit. He would not let anything come in the way of what he wanted to do with his life, not even risks. One of the most important lessons you will learn as a hard-worker is that risks become less important when you are now ready

The Fervent Tenacity of an Inventor/Innovator

be very diligent to achieve your God-given goals. When you work hard enough, risks can be smartly calculated and drastically minimized.

Ford was ready to put in all the work required to get to where he had desired and foreseen his life was headed. To the young Henry Ford, it was not just about the talent that he had; he knew that for anyone to amount to anything great in life, he or she has to put in the required work. Over the next two-and-half years he held several jobs, sometimes moving when he thought he could learn more somewhere else. His most important motive of working at any job was to rigorously devour any form of knowledge that would be useful in doing the thing he really loved to do.

It is disheartening to see lack of tenacity in many people that have resigned their lives to work at jobs they do not really like just for the purpose of earning money. How do you expect to be positioned as an inventor or an innovator if all you use your life to do is to be imprisoned by the job-salary system? Yes Ford started with working at jobs but his sole purpose was to discover the genius capability within him; he was always dreaming of how he wanted to change the world with inventions and innovations. He knew that innovative and inventive ideas would not just fall on his laps if he would not go get the necessary knowledge and skills required to nurture his creativity to productivity levels that are irrefutable.

I like to give you a sound advice — If you still feel the need to remain in the job-salary system, make sure you are in a position where you can add maximum value to yourself, even as you are serving the needs of the company you are working with. Make sure your job is the one that is continually allowing you to discover the exceedingly great potentials that are resident within you; all the value added to you when you work at a job will be an investment that will contribute to the great things you will eventually do in life with your creative, innovative, and inventive proficiency. Believe me that it takes audacious tenacity to sometimes leave a high-paying job for a lower-paying job just because the less lucrative job will afford you the opportunity of growing yourself to become the person you were really created to be.

Ford was back home in 1882 but he chose not to focus his attention on farming activities. Instead, he serviced and operated portable steam engines used by farmers, and sometimes worked in factories in Detroit; he cut and sold timber from 40 acres of his father's land. At this point, Ford was validating his tenacious attitude while beginning to realize that the time to start working for himself rather than being somebody's employee was around the corner.

In 1888 Ford married Clara Bryant and because of marital responsibilities, in 1891 they moved to Detroit where Henry had to take a job again as night engineer for the Edison Electric Illuminating Company. Ford just knew a little bit about electricity but he saw the job again as an opportunity to learn, in addition to taking care of some financial needs. Ford had a very industrious personality and by 1896 he became the chief engineer of the Illuminating Company. However, he had other interests and he made sure he found time for the things he badly wanted to do. He was helped by a group of friends to start conducting some experiments, and these crowned the year 1896 with the accomplishment of his first self-propelled vehicle, the Quadricycle.

The Fervent Tenacity of an Inventor/Innovator

Wow! Ford eventually made it. Though, it had taken several years of tenacious hard work but his dreams started becoming physical manifestation. He got to the point of his first product completion. It was the dawning of a new day for him; he had little doubt that his name was soon going to be listed among the world's foremost innovators and inventors of all time. If he had not been doggedly resolute, the inventor in him would not have manifested; he gave it all it took at least to come up with his first invention.

Have you realized that Ford was not giving excuses that condone any inability to become who he was created to be? Many people today are priding themselves in the flimsy excuses of things not working well for them, and that is why they cannot begin to create, innovate, and invent. In fact, one of the best reasons to start inventing is because things are not working well and you want to turn the situation of things around, not only for yourself but for as many people as possible.

Do you think it was Ford's utmost desire to be hopping from job to job? Don't you think that just like everybody else, he would have loved to have most of the things needed for the kind of inventions he had in mind at his door steps? The fact of life is that the great things we earnestly desire don't come so easily. They come with a price, and this price is the tenacity that it requires to overcome challenges and limitations that are stopping others from maximizing their potentials. Ford did not forget about his inventions while working at different jobs; he saw them as a way of paying the price for what he really loved to do. The price of world-changing innovations and inventions is a winning attitude that makes sure you are sedulously prepared and not ready to rest until all you are born to do is accomplished.

His tenacity was really paying off as he released his second car in 1898. Ford needed to do the hard work of clearly articulating his vision to others and he had to pass through the rigor of convincing people to join him and help him achieve his dream. He persuaded a group of businessmen to back him in the biggest risk of his life — a company to make and sell horseless carriages. Don't you think you may also need to develop great persuasive skills in order to make the innovations and inventions you are seeing in your mind get to the lime light where it can be of immense benefit to all and sundry? The art of developing the necessary skills is only going to happen through WORK. The reason why many people have not been able to bless the world in the way their hearts truly desire is because they have refused to do the hard work required to convincingly assure and influence the people that will help them carry out the great vision that will birth the inventions and innovations they were destined to create.

FAILURE IS AN OPPORTUNITY

Failure is only an opportunity to, more intelligently begin again.
HENRY FORD

Unfortunately, the first two cars that Ford produced did not succeed in the market. This was because Ford knew nothing about running a business, and learning by trial-and-error always involves failure, yet he was still determined because he knew failure is only an opportunity to more intelligently begin again, and to do it better than what was previously

The Fervent Tenacity of an Inventor/Innovator

done. Fear of failure was not strong enough to deter him from his purpose. Ford started two companies that failed — What an ugly situation he went through!

Do you know that this seemingly discouraging situation that Ford passed through would have sent some others back to the job-salary system, never to try to invent again? But Ford was resolute; he was audaciously tenacious — he decided to recover his fortunes; he still kept on taking bigger risks, building and even driving racing cars.

Eventually, Ford had success. It is indeed true that people who don't quit eventually win. The new cars he began producing found success and these attracted additional financial backers to him. This led him to incorporate his third automotive venture, Ford Motor Company on June 16, 1903. His success was so huge that he could easily sell all he could make; meeting demand was now the challenge — how great it is to create world-changing inventions!

He had some early cars that didn't sell well, the Ford Model B, the Ford Model K. They were not sales triumphs. He had some innovations that he tried to do. He had what he called the X-Engine. It was an eight-cylinder engine with the cylinders in the shape of an X. They worked on that thing for years and it never worked out. But, failure was not something that he was afraid of, in fact, he has a, slightly awkwardly phrased line:

> *If I fail and I can analyze the failure and figure it out why I failed, why, then maybe I can be a success. But if I don't try, then I'll never be a success; I'll never achieve anything.*
> Henry Ford

And so, failure was not something that he was particularly afraid of. Look at the record of any innovative person. They've all got things they tried to do that just didn't work out. But, if they don't keep trying, they're not going to find the one that does work out. So, that was Ford's philosophy and, he simply was not afraid to try something and fail.

Every time of failure for you is supposed to be a time of important and valuable lessons; but you will not realize that your failure is an opportunity to become better at what you do if you don't know how to do the hard work of detailed analysis of the factors, the causes and effects of the failure (just like Ford said in his quote above), and make sure you convert each of your mistakes and shortcomings to a great success for yourself and your world that will be a beneficiary of your inventions and innovations.

When some people achieve some level of success, they begin to relax and forget that the best is yet to come. But the tenacity of Ford's hard work would not let him rest — he badly wanted to make all the cars he could sell. Doing that required a bigger factory. In 1910 the company moved into a huge new plant in the north of Detroit at Highland Park, Michigan. Again, Ford Motor Company commenced an unyielding drive to intensify production and reduce costs. Ford and his team copied concepts from gun manufacturers, watch producers, bicycle makers, and meat packers. The borrowed concepts were mixed with their own ideas and by late 1913, they had developed a revolutionary moving assembly line for automobiles. That was a wonderful innovation that changed the history of the automobile industry forever.

The Fervent Tenacity of an Inventor/Innovator

Friend, it is only hard work in relentless tenacity that can bring the best of your genius abilities out of you. Even when people are praising you for the wonderful things you are doing, if you are not a tenacious person, you may begin to become complacent. But the people who have understood that there are so many capabilities in them yet to be discovered and utilized keep striving hard without the fear of failure to bless their world in the maximum possible way.

TENACITY TO OVERCOME FAILURE

One of the most prolific inventors of all time, Thomas Edison has over 1,090 United States patents, along with many others in countries like France, Germany, and the UK; he just couldn't stop coming up with new and innovative inventions. His creations are some of the most impactful of his and future generations; electrical power, affordable filament-based light bulbs, motion picture, and sound recording amongst many others. The whole world knows how successful an inventor Edison was, however, very few people know the true story behind Edison's success. Thomas Edison failed more times than most people, but he never gave up; he invested time and money, and lost, but it didn't dissuade him. He didn't perceive failure like most people do and he was famously quoted as saying,

> *Just because something doesn't do what you planned it to do doesn't mean it's useless.*
> THOMAS EDISON

Whenever a promising venture does not go as planned, rather than let his head drop in despair, Edison would count his losses, and think of ways the failed invention could be put to profitable use. Edison once delved into mining in the bid to ease the scarcity of high-grade iron-ore in the United States in the late 1890s. The mining company failed, but Edison took the equipment he used for the mining to start cement production. After completion of his cement factory, the product was too expensive and many couldn't afford it, instead of shutting up shop, Edison secured a contract to build the Yankees stadium in Bronx and his cement was finally put to good use. He never believed in failure, and in every setback, he saw an opportunity to create something else.

This mentality can be traced to his childhood. Growing up, Edison was deemed too difficult to teach and as a result, he only had about 3 months of formal education before he was withdrawn from school. For most people, getting thrown out of school would be seen as a monumental setback, but it wasn't so for Edison. His mother trained him for a while and as soon as he could read, he developed a love for studying; this helped him a lot on his way to becoming the inventor that he ended up being. So, we have a boy that didn't receive the formal education that many of his mates received; a boy that was home-schooled and self-schooled; in reality, Edison wasn't on to the very best of starts.

When he was 12-years old, he sold newspapers on the railroad to make extra cash, and taking advantage of his access to the railroad cars; he set up a laboratory in a train baggage car and started conducting experiments. One day, a chemical he was using for his experiment caught fire and he nearly burned the car; because of this, he was sent off the

THE FERVENT TENACITY OF AN INVENTOR/INNOVATOR

cars and he had to sell his wares from station to station. Did Edison give up on chemical experiments from then on? Of course not, he just looked for another location to continue his experiments.

After some time, he read up on electrical science and it intrigued him so much that he decided to examine and experiment on electricity. While trying to perfect a way to provide electricity to the masses, Edison would try repeatedly and fail, but he never stopped trying. On occasions, he'd run out of money to fund his research and run his laboratory, but, rather than give up on his dream, Edison would suspend work on that project, and come up with a smaller invention that he would sell, then use the proceeds to fund his main work; which was making electricity available for all. On his way to building the first affordable and efficient filament-based light bulb, Edison was said to have failed 10,000 times before getting it right. When asked about it, he said, *"I have not failed, I've just found 10,000 ways that won't work."* After his success with the light bulb in 1880, he began work in earnest to build a company that would have the capability to deliver electricity to every city in the world.

How many times have you failed at a particular endeavour before you gave up on it? Was it 10 times? A hundred? Definitely not a thousand times. Edison failed ten thousand times and still didn't give up. Now imagine if he'd given up at his first hurdle (the learning difficulty that meant he had to be home-schooled), would he have been able to achieve all that he did? How will the world be without his over 1,000 inventions? Would the world know the name Thomas Edison, or will he just be another child that didn't amount to anything? The only people who have never failed are those

The Creative and Innovative Power of a Genius

who have never tried, and if you hope to be the creator our Creator created you to be, then you must be prepared to face hurdles and scale them; it is in the scaling of these hurdles that the achievement of your goals lie; it is only by scaling them you can fully develop your creative potential.

> *To make our way, we must have firm resolve, persistence, tenacity.*
> **Ralph Bunche**

As the quote above states, to accomplish anything of note in your life, you need tenacity, and perseverance and to reach your goals, you must have a steely resolve and an enduring persistence. You don't just quit because things are not playing out the way you planned. To successfully invent or create anything of note, you must always try one more time as said in Edison's quote below. If the person with a ground-breaking and innovative idea — in the world has not been faced with failure at one time or the other, then what sets inventors apart from pretenders? When it comes to inventions and innovations, what separates the men from the boys is the ability to shake-off the failure and forge ahead.

> *Our greatest weakness lies in giving up. The most certain way to succeed is always to try just one more time.*
> **Thomas Edison**

When Cletus Ibeto was 13-years old, his father, realizing that he couldn't afford to keep all his sons at school, decided that Cletus would have to drop out and learn a trade while his two brothers continued at school. Imagine the sadness

The Fervent Tenacity of an Inventor/Innovator

he must have felt, a 13-year old, being told that he had to be the sacrificial lamb, the one left behind. He was sad and he rebelled against the decision by refusing to eat, and afterwards, pleading with his father to reconsider; his father didn't. Cletus was sent to Onitsha for his apprenticeship, and while there, he was mocked endlessly for his fate. At age 17, and preparing to go into business on his own, the Nigerian civil war broke out, meaning he had to join the military.

After the war, he started petty trading and from that time, things began to look up for him. Cletus Ibeto looked around him and saw a need; cars were beginning to make their way into Nigeria, but when these cars got faulty, spare parts weren't available to fix them. As a result, some of the cars had to be sent to dealerships in faraway states. Ibeto started importing motor vehicle spare parts and he made a fortune doing so. With the money he made from importing spare parts, Ibeto built the largest locally-owned spare parts manufacturing plant in the country; this meant he didn't have to import the parts anymore, he built them here himself. Today, Cletus is a billionaire and one of the most influential men in the country.

> *Let me tell you something that has led me to my goal. My strength lies ...in my tenacity.*
> LOUIS PASTEUR

Imagine, a boy that was deemed not good enough for school turning out to be a business genius. Starting out with nothing like he did, can you imagine how much hardship he must have encountered? But his strength was his tenacity, just as Louis Pasteur said in his quote above; he

The Creative and Innovative Power of a Genius

never gave up and didn't look back. Today, he is not only a wealthy and well-respected man; he has created jobs for, and impacted the life of many Nigerians. What if he chose to dwell on the fact that his father didn't think he was good enough for school? Or if he had let the civil war derail his goals of being a successful businessman? He would have ended up like many before him and after him. What setback have you been dwelling on? What failure is holding you back? To become a successful creator or inventor, you must be tenacious enough to shrug off the failure and become who you were destined to be.

> *Do not give up your dreams because it is apparently not being realized...cling to your vision with all the tenacity you can muster.*
> ORION SWETT MARDEN

Another person that used failure as a raw material for invention is Innocent Chukwuma, who applied to study Engineering but he was rejected. He did not give up on his dreams; he firmly clung to all the tenacity he could gather. Today, he is the founder of Innoson Motors, the first and only Nigerian company that manufactures motor vehicles. How did he start? As a young man, Innocent wanted to dabble into motorcycle importation and sales, but he saw that the money used in importing said motorcycles meant that they were sold at a premium. Innocent wondered why the shipping costs were so high and he decided to travel abroad to the seaport that the motorcycles were sent from to do an investigation. His rejection from the school of engineering was about to become his raw material for success. On getting there, he found out why; one motorcycle was loaded wholly

THE FERVENT TENACITY OF AN INVENTOR/INNOVATOR

into a crate, and the crate, loaded on the ship, meaning, if 50 motorcycles were to be shipped, 50 crates would be used.

Seeing this, he was hit by insight, Innocent looked at the problem and saw a great opportunity. He went back home with crates of motorcycles and started selling his own products at 40% less than the usual price. Do you know what the brilliant young man did? He asked that the motorcycles be uncoupled and packed in the crate, by doing so, each crate could now contain 5 uncoupled motorcycles, and on getting to Nigeria, Innocent would couple the motorcycles and sell at unbeatable prices. Genius! Rather than use 50 crates to import 50 motorcycles like his peers were doing, Innocent only needed 10 crates; this slashed a substantial amount off the shipping bill, and he could then afford to flourish at the business.

With the fortune he made from the motorcycle business, Innocent started his own plastic factory. Why? He noticed how many plastic parts the motorcycles he imported had, and he decided to start producing them locally, that way, he only had to import the non-plastic parts, thereby further reducing importation costs and creating a new business opportunity for himself. Shortly after, his fellow businessmen started to import only the non-plastic parts too and guess who they bought the plastic parts from? Innocent.

Denied admission, Innocent didn't dwell on it, he started selling spare parts. When he wanted to trade up and start selling motorcycles, he saw a challenge — high costs — and decided to do something about it. He could have seen the issue as insurmountable like many of his peers did, but Innocent knew that problems/failures were nothing but stepping stones to greatness, and rather than settle for less, he came up with a brilliant idea that revolutionized motorcycle importation in Nigeria. Today, he has many companies and employs thousands of Nigerians; the same man who couldn't afford the capital for what was then a mainstream business.

What problem is holding you back from realizing your inventiveness today? Is it failure? I have just shown you a man that failed thousands of times without giving up? Is it lack of money? Innocent Chukwuma didn't grow up in a very privileged home, neither did Cletus Ibeto, yet they were able to accomplish great feats. You must know that the only thing holding you back is yourself. Do you want to tap into the greatness you have been blessed with? Do you want to come up with creations, innovative ideas that will shake the world? Then you must adopt the tenacity of inventors. You cannot let problems or failures weigh you down, you cannot be blindsided by setbacks or challenges. No one has ever become an inventor by giving up halfway through. Like the great man, Thomas Edison once said,

> *Many of life's failures are people who did not realize how close they were to success when they gave up.*
> THOMAS EDISON

Will you give up only to realise you were so close to your goal, or will you try one more time? Edison tried one more time, and today, he is regarded as the greatest inventor of all time. No matter the amount of treasures you have discovered within yourself, if you will not tenaciously work hard to bring all your desires into physical manifestation, you may not be able to deliver all the inventions and creations you were created to bless your world with.

GOLDEN NUGGETS
FROM CHAPTER 12

- Inventions and innovations require self-confidence, a taste for taking risks, leadership ability and a vision of what the future should be.

- If you still feel the need to remain in the job-salary system, make sure you are in a position where you can add maximum value to yourself, even as you are serving the needs of the company you are working with.

- It takes audacious tenacity to sometimes leave a high-paying job for a lower-paying job just because the less lucrative job will afford you the opportunity of growing yourself to become the person you were really created to be.

- The price of world-changing innovations and inventions is a winning attitude that makes sure you are sedulously prepared and not ready to rest until all you are born to do is accomplished.

- Every time of failure for you is supposed to be a time of important and valuable lessons; but you will not realize that your failure is an opportunity to become better at what you do if you don't know how to do the hard work of detailed analysis of the factors, the causes and effects of the failure.

- It is only hard work in relentless tenacity that can bring the best of your genius abilities out of you. Even when people are praising you for the wonderful things you are doing, if you are not a tenacious person, you may begin to become complacent.

- The people who have understood that there are so many capabilities in them yet to be discovered and utilized keep striving hard without the fear of failure to bless their world in the maximum possible way.

- The only people who have never failed are those who have never tried, and if you hope to be the creator our Creator created you to be, then you must be prepared to face hurdles and scale them; it is in the scaling of these hurdles that the achievement of your goals lie; it is only by scaling them you can fully develop your creative potential.

- To successfully invent or create anything of note, you must always try one more time after each failure.

- When it comes to inventions and innovations, what separates the men from the boys is the ability to shake-off the failure and forge ahead.

- No one has ever become an inventor by giving up halfway through.

- No matter the amount of treasures you have discovered within yourself, if you will not tenaciously work hard to bring all your desires into physical manifestation, you may not be able to deliver all the inventions and creations you were created to bless your world with.

FINAL THOUGHTS

I like to say congratulations to you if you have read the entire book in your hands. The keys to unlocking all the genius potentials and abilities in you have just been given to you. But it will be very beneficial for you if you take time to read the book over and over so that you are actually getting to apply the principles therein, and do not stop until you have delivered to your world everything you were created to accomplish.

The Creator put so much of these blessings in you so that you can be a blessing to as many people as possible. One major characteristic of every great genius, innovator, inventor and creator that should be conspicuously evident in your life from now on is hard work. Without hard work, you will never amount to anything substantial in life. Outside of diligence, there is no chance for you to remove yourself from the society of nonentities. Only being industrious will elevate you to a position where you can stand as a champion before kings and rulers of this world in different spheres of life.

As from now on, never allow anyone to treat you as someone without value; never accept the life of mediocrity, no matter how widely people are embracing it. Choose to be different by doing all the work required and giving it all it takes to discover all the latent potentials, abilities, and talents within you and be diligent enough to maximize them

The Creative and Innovative Power of a Genius

for the beneficial use of humanity. Let your life prove to mankind that God created everybody as a genius but only those who choose to develop their own ability, and consequently convert their potentials into useful inventions and innovations are acknowledged and celebrated by all. Accept yourself as who you are — you are a genius; you are destined to create, innovate, and invent!

REFERENCES

1. https://greennews.ng/campus-hero-ufot-ekong-who-made-landmark-records-at-japanese-university/

2. nigerianuniversityscholarships.com/5-nigerian-geniuses-you-should-know/

3. www.recordsng.com/2014/12/about-aliko-dangote-biography-Profile-Family-Children.html?m=1

4. pointblanknews.com/pbn/exclusive/nigerian-math-genius-esther-okade-starts-university-uk-10/

5. https://en.m.wikipedia.org/wiki/Stephen_Hawking

6. https://en.m.wikipedia.org/wiki/Alexander_Animalu

7. businessnews.com.ng/2011/11/01/house-of-tara-orekelewa-story-of-the-makeup-genius/

8. www.encylclpedia.com/people/medicine/medicine-biographies/benjamin-s-carson

9. www.nairaland.com/2502109/pains-first-class-graduate-nigeria

10. www.nationalhelm.net/2016/06/please-help-unemployed-first-class.html?m=1

11. www.naij.com/tag/folorunsho_alakija.html

12. dailypost.ng/2016/11/03/firs-recruitment-700000-applied-500-jobs/

13. Dangote (https://en.wikipedia.org/wiki/Aliko-Dangote)

14. Nigerian Bureau of Statistics (www.nigerianstat.gov.ng/library#content5-6)

15. Malawian boy (www.ted.com/talks/william-kamkwamba-how-i-harnessed-the-word?language=en)

16. Mark Zuckerberg (https://zephoria.com/top-15-valuable-facebook-statistics/)

17. http://westchester.libraryreserve.com/10/50/en/ContentDetails.htm?id=C9A87E0D-3517-44FB-8346-1C93C8986C2A

18. https://www.businessinsider.com/5-of-albert-einstein-thought-experiments-that-revolutionized-science-2016-7?

19. punchng.com/nigerias-unemployment-rate-rises-13-3-nbs/

20. www.biography.com/people/isaac-newton-9422656

21. www.goodreads.com/quotes/tag/thinking

22. news.harvard.edu/gazette/story/2013/09/dawn-of-a-revolution/

23. qz.com/668514/if-you-want-to-be-like-warren-buffett-and-bill-gates-adopt-their-voraciuos-reading-habits/

24. uk.businessinsider.com/rich-people-like-to-read-2105-8?r=US&IR=T

25. http://www.biography.com/people/ben-carson-475422#

References

26. http://www.biography.com/people/elon-musk

27. www.gatesnotes.com

28. https://en.m.wikipedia.org/wiki/Oprah_Book_Club

29. https://en.m.wikipedia.org/wiki/Mark_Zuckerberg_book_club

30. buzznigeria.com/richest-men-nigeria/

31. https://en.m.wikipedia.org/wiki/Theophilus_Danjuma

32. www.nairaland.com/3349433/10/ridiculous-things-nigeria-imports

33. dailypost.ng/2016/-2/-1/nigeria-to-start-producing-own-pencils-by-2018-onu/

34. https://en.m.wikipedia.org/wiki/Taiwo_Akinkumi

35. www.tori.ng/news/8152/so-sad-the-tale-of-pa-taiwo-akinkumi-the-man-who.html

36. buzznigeria.com/richest-men-nigeria/

37. www.nairaland.com/3201279/take-advantage-great-opportunity

38. www.goaldig.com/Aliko-Dangote-Quotes.html

39. https://en.m.wikipedia.org/wiki/Elon_Musk

40. www.thisdaylive.com/index.php/2016/07/09/nnamdi-ezeigbo-my-grass-to-grace-story-of-slot-group

41. http://thinkers50.com/blog/innovation-leonardo-da-vinci/

42. dynamicpedia.com/2016/01/09/worlds-most-innovative-inventions-by-manoj-bhargava-life-of-billions-of-people-about-to-change/

43. techland.time.com/2015/05/03/math-genius-solves-100-year-old-problem-then-refuses-million-dollar-prize/

44. http://charlessledge.com/the-importance-of-solitude/

45. www.postcolonialweb.org/soyinka/ake/lpg1.html

46. www.thefamouspeople.com/profiles/wole-soyinka-3329.php

47. www.livescience.com/41780-washington-carver-html

48. https://en.m.wikipedia.org/wiki/Nikola_Tesla

49. www.brainyquotes.com

50. startupdaily.com/success-story-of-innocent-chukwuma/

51. startupdaily.com/success-story-cletus-ibeto/

52. www.biography.com/people/thomas-edison-9284349#

53. https://en.m.wikipedia.org/wiki/Thomas_Edison

54. www.nairaland.com/2994514/16-nigerian-inventors-remarkable-inventions

55. anonhq.com/10-most-intelligent-people-alive-today/

56. en.m.wikipedia.org/wiki/Michael-Faraday

57. www.kidinventorsday.com/quotes.htm

58. https://www.linkedin.com/cyprian-emeka-uzoh

SUNDAY ADELAJA'S BIOGRAPHY

Pastor Sunday Adelaja is the Founder and Senior Pastor of The Embassy of the Blessed Kingdom of God for All Nations Church in Kyiv, Ukraine.

Sunday Adelaja is a Nigerian-born Leader, Thinker, Philosopher, Transformation Strategist, Pastor, Author and Innovator who lives in Kiev, Ukraine.

At 19, he won a scholarship to study in the former Soviet Union. He completed his master's program in Belorussia State University with distinction in journalism.

At 33, he had built the largest evangelical church in Europe — The Embassy of the Blessed Kingdom of God for All Nations.

Sunday Adelaja is one of the few individuals in our world who has been privileged to speak in the United Nations, Israeli Parliament, Japanese Parliament and the United States Senate.

The movement he pioneered has been instrumental in reshaping lives of people in the Ukraine, Russia and about 50 other nations where he has his branches.

His congregation, which consists of ninety-nine percent white Europeans, is a cross-cultural model of the church for the 21st century.

His life mission is to advance the Kingdom of God on earth by raising a generation of history makers who will live for a cause larger, bigger and greater than themselves. Those who will live like Jesus and transform every sphere of the society in every nation as a model of the Kingdom of God on earth.

His economic empowerment program has succeeded in raising over 200 millionaires in the short period of three years.

Sunday Adelaja is the author of over 300 books, many of which are translated into several languages including Russian, English, French, Chinese, German, etc.

His work has been widely reported by world media outlets such as The Washington Post, The Wall Street Journal, New York Times, Forbes, Associated Press, Reuters, CNN, BBC, German, Dutch and French national television stations.

Pastor Sunday is happily married to his "Princess" Bose Dere-Adelaja. They are blessed with three children: Perez, Zoe and Pearl.

Bill Clinton —
42Nd President Of The United States (1993–2001), Former Arcansas State Governor

Ariel "Arik" Sharon — Israeli Politician, Israeli Prime Minister (2001–2006)

Benjamin Netanyahu — Statesman Of Israel. Israeli Prime Minister (1996–1999), Acting Prime Minister (From 2009)

Jean ChrEtien —
Canadian Politician,
20[Th] Prime Minister Of
Canada, Minister Of Justice
Of Canada, Head Of Liberan
Party Of Canada

Rudolph Giuliani —
American Political Actor,
Mayor Of New York Served
From 1994 To 2001. Actor
Of Republican Party

Colin Powell —
Is An American Statesman
And A Retired Four-Star
General In The Us Army,
65[Th] United States Secretary
Of State

Peter J. Daniels —
Is A Well-Known And
Respected Australian
Christian International
Business Statesman Of
Substance

Madeleine
Korbel Albright —
An American Politician And
Diplomat, 64th United States
Secretary Of State

Kenneth Robert
Livingstone —
An English Politician,
1st Mayor Of London
(4 May 2000 – 4 May
2008), Labour Party
Representative

Sir Richard Charles Nicholas Branson — English Business Magnate, Investor And Philanthropist. He Founded The *Virgin Group*, Which Controls More Than 400 Companies

Mel Gibson — American Actor And Filmmaker

Chuck Norris — American Martial Artist, Actor, Film Producer And Screenwriter

Christopher Tucker — American Actor And Comedian

Bernice Albertine King — American Minister Best Known As The Youngest Child Of Civil Rights Leaders Martin Luther King Jr. And Coretta Scott King Andrew

Andrew Young — American Politician, Diplomat, And Activist, 14Th United States Ambassador To The United Nations, 55Th Mayor Of Atlanta

General Wesley Kanne Clark — 4-Star General And Nato Supreme Allied Commander

Dr. Sunday Adelaja's family:
Perez, Pearl, Zoe and Pastor Bose Adelaja

FOLLOW SUNDAY ADELAJA ON SOCIAL MEDIA

Subscribe And Read Pastor Sunday's Blog:
www.sundayadelajablog.com

Follow these links and listen to over 200 of Pastor Sunday's Messages free of charge:
http://sundayadelajablog.com/content/

Follow Pastor Sunday on Twitter:
www.twitter.com/official_pastor

Join Pastor Sunday's Facebook page to stay in touch:
www.facebook.com/pastor.sunday.adelaja

Visit our websites for more information about Pastor Sunday's ministry:
http://www.godembassy.com
http://www.pastorsunday.com
http://sundayadelaja.de

CONTACT

FOR DISTRIBUTION OR TO ORDER
BULK COPIES OF THIS BOOK,
PLEASE CONTACT US:

USA
CORNERSTONE PUBLISHING
info@thecornerstonepublishers.com
+1 (516) 547-4999
www.thecornerstonepublishers.com

AFRICA
SUNDAY ADELAJA MEDIA LTD.
E-mail: btawolana@hotmail.com
+2348187518530, +2348097721451, +2348034093699

LONDON, UK
PASTOR ABRAHAM GREAT
abrahamagreat@gmail.com
+447711399828, +441908538141

KIEV, UKRAINE
pa@godembassy.org
Mobile: +380674401958

Best Selling Books by Dr. Sunday Adelaja
Available on Amazon.com and Okadabooks.com

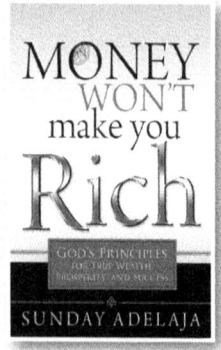
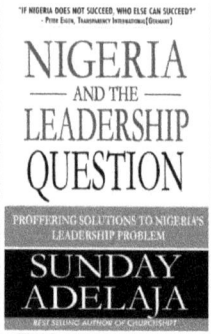

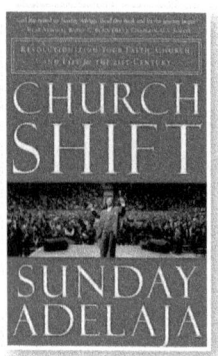
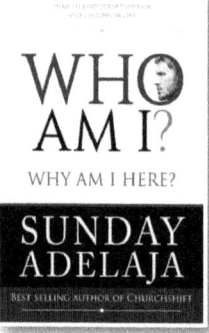

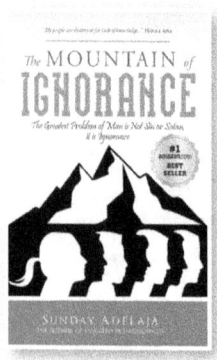

BEST SELLING BOOKS BY DR. SUNDAY ADELAJA
AVAILABLE ON AMAZON.COM AND OKADABOOKS.COM

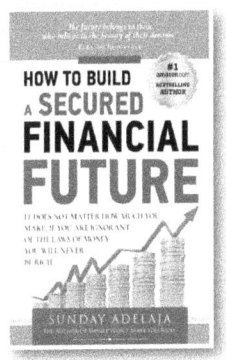

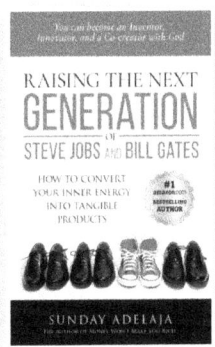

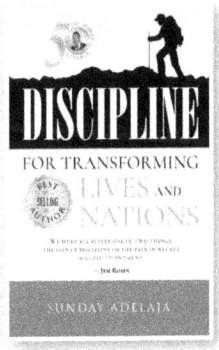
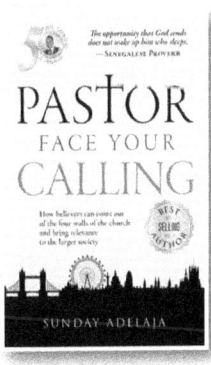

GOLDEN JUBILEE SERIES BOOKS
BY DR. SUNDAY ADELAJA

1. Who Am I
2. Only God Can Save Nigeria
3. The Mountain Of Ignorance
4. Stop Working For Uncle Sam
5. Poverty Mindset Vs Abundance Mindset
6. Raising The Next Generation Of Steve Jobs And Bill Gates
7. How To Build A Secured Financial Future
8. How To Become Great Through Time Conversion
9. Create Your Own Net Worth
10. Why You Must Urgently Become A Workaholic
11. How To Regain Your Lost Years
12. Pastor, Face Your Calling
13. Discipline For Transforming Lives And Nations
14. Excellence Your Key To Elevation
15. No One Is Better Than You
16. Problems Your Shortcut To Prominence
17. Let Heroes Arise!
18. How To Live An Effective Life
19. How To Win In Life
20. The Creative And Innovative Power Of A Genius
21. The Veritable Source Of Energy
22. The Nigerian Economy. The Way Forward
23. How To Get What You Need In Life
24. 7 Tips To Self-Fulfillment
25. Life Is An Opportunity
26. The Essence And Value Of Life
27. A Visionless Life Is A Meaningless Life
28. Where There Is Problem There Is Money
29. Work Is Better Than Vacation, Labour Better Than Favour
30. How To Overcome The Fear Of Death
31. Discovering The Purpose And Calling Of Nations
32. How To Become A Developed Nation Throught The Dignity Of Labor
33. Your Greatnes Is Proportional
34. Why Losing Your Job Is The Best Thing That Could Happen To You
35. What Do You Do With Your Time
36. Life Is Predictable
37. How To Be In The Here And Now
38. I Am A Person. Am I A Personality?
39. Discover The Source Of Your Latent Energy
40. How To Form Value Systems In A Child
41. Why I Am Unlucky
42. Hello! I Am Searching For Problems
43. Holistic Personality
44. How To transform And Build a Civilized Nation
45. Could You Be The Abraham Of Your Nation
46. The teambuilding skills of Jesus
47. How to keep your focus
48. The sin of irresponsibility
49. How Africans Brought Civilization To Europe
50. The Danger Of Monoculturalism

FOR DISTRIBUTION OR TO ORDER BULK COPIES OF THIS BOOKS, PLEASE CONTACT US:
USA | CORNERSTONE PUBLISHING
  E-mail: info@thecornerstonepublishers.com, +1 (516) 547-4999
  www.thecornerstonepublishers.com
AFRICA | SUNDAY ADELAJA MEDIA LTD.
  E-mail: btawolana@hotmail.com
  +2348187518530, +2348097721451, +2348034093699
LONDON, UK | PASTOR ABRAHAM GREAT
  E-mail: abrahamagreat@gmail.com, +447711399828, +441908538141
KIEV, UKRAINE |
  E-mail: pa@godembassy.org, Mobile: +380674401958

www.ingramcontent.com/pod-product-compliance
Lightning Source LLC
Chambersburg PA
CBHW060457090426
42735CB00011B/2022